# Daily groove

## a big, fat, scary devotional

SCOTT MAUCK

THOMAS NELSON BIBLES
NASHVILLE
A DIVISION OF THOMAS NELSON, INC.
www.ThomasNelson.com
www.Xt4J.com

Published in Nashville, Tennessee, by Thomas Nelson, Inc.

Extreme for Jesus™ Brand Manager: Hayley Morgan
Extreme for Jesus™ Acquisitions Editor: Kate Etue

Cover Design: Pointsize Associates, Glasgow, Scotland

Scripture quotations are from THE NEW KING JAMES VERSION, copyright © 1979, 1980, 1982, Thomas Nelson, Inc., Publishers and from THE NEW CENTURY VERSION, copyright © 1987, 1988, 1991 by W. Publishing, a division of Thomas Nelson, Inc.

**Library of Congress Cataloging-in-Publication Data**
Mauck, Scott, 1965—
    Daily groove : a big fat scary devotional / Scott Mauck.
      p. cm.
   ISBN 0-7180-0086-2
   1. Teenage boys—Prayer-books and devotions—English. 2. Christian teenagers—Prayer-books and devotions—English. 3. Devotional calendars. I. Title.

BV4855 .M38 2002
242'.632—dc21                           2001044897

*Printed in the United States of America.*
02 03 04 05 06 PHX 5 4 3 2 1

Two people are better than one, because they get more done by working together. If one falls down, the other can help him up. But it is bad for the person who is alone and falls, because no one is there to help. > > > > > > > > > > > > > > > > > > >

You've been planning this jam all day. You and your friend have been talking about it non-stop. You didn't know he could play guitar! After school, when you finally start to jam, you realize that he can't play at all. Instead of giving him some pointers, you tell him he's an idiot for even thinking he could play. He, on the other hand, just wanted to learn a little more. He knew he wasn't very good and now you've made him not even want to try.

We are fickle people. Often, even though we want people to be all God wants them to be, we can't wait for 'em to mess up so we can exploit their mistake and put them down. We can't have it both ways. In encouraging others, we have to do it even when we don't feel comfortable, or we don't feel like they deserve it. Truth is, you probably won't find a good friend if you can't be one. Do you agree?

So Jesus was not able to work any miracles there except to heal a few sick people by putting his hands on them. He was amazed at how many people had no faith. >>>>>>>>>>>>>>

School projects are always work. This one, however, has been the hardest project all year. You're working frantically when you look at the clock and realize you have been at it for six hours. You're really proud of your work—it's probably the best paper you've written. You figure that you have about two more hours until you're done. Right before you run your last spell check, the power goes out, and you haven't saved.

# Ugghh!

You just want to scream. Now what? The paper is due in the morning and there is no way you can get it done. You are so mad, but who can you blame? There really isn't anybody. Sometimes we have no control over events. None whatsoever. When Jesus was faced with this He moved on and continued ministry. So move on. Make your case with your teacher and see what happens.

## >> Ephesians 4:29

When you talk, do not say harmful things, but say what people need—words that will help others become stronger. Then what you say will do good to those who listen to you. > > > > > > > > > > > > >

Try this: Start every conversation over the next three days by saying something that will majorly make someone's day. Sound easy? Maybe not. I tried it with some guy friends and I couldn't believe how hard it was to come up with something. The normal convo' is stuff like, "Hey, butthead," "You're wearing that?," or "Bro', do you know how stupid you sound?" Putting each other down has become the thing to do. Guess we do it to make ourselves feel better, but we don't even realize it 'til we try to be nice. So what's up with God on this? He says we are supposed to be building people up, not tearing them down.

So give it a try, I dare ya. It might not be as easy as you think, but watch how people react. It'll be a trip.

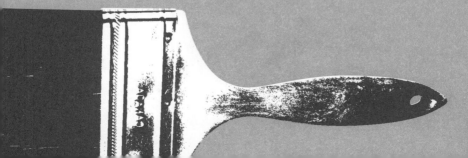

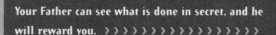
## >> Matthew 6:6b

It's all set up. This is going to be your claim to fame. You'll jump off the roof, land on the trampoline, do two flips, and land head-first in the pool. And your best bud will capture it on video, so you can send it to one of those reality shows. On top of the wad you'll win, this will be your fifteen minutes of fame. After this, that hotty will be yours. To her, you will be a star.

Screetch! We interrupt this fantasy for a word from our Savior. You got it all wrong. You think you need to risk death to impress? It's actually the opposite. It's the stuff you do without getting noticed that really counts. But it's harder. Maybe even harder than jumping off the roof. You think you're man enough to try it?

What does it mean to have a full life? Doing everything humanly possible before you die? Backpacking across Europe? Winning *Survivor*?

For centuries people have tried to answer this question: "How do I fill this hole?" And you know what they've found? Doing more is never enough. There's always something else to do. The void inside still remains empty. After Europe, there's Africa. Even fame doesn't do it. Suicide, drugs, fast cars—stars try all they can to feel better.

So how do you do it? How do you fill the hole? Jesus had an answer that may be the hardest thing you'll ever do, but it is the only thing that will take away the pain. Love somebody. Love God. Simple? Not really. But worth it? It's the only thing that will fill that hole. Risk it. Get life to the full.

My sheep listen to my voice; I know them, and they follow me. >>>>>>>>>>>>>>>>>>>>>>>>

It seemed pretty harmless at the time. It wasn't something you looked forward to anyway, but Mom and Dad insisted that you be there, then gave you the famous "you-will-be-on-your-best-behavior" speech. So instead of hanging with the fam', you took off with your cousin to make your own fun. You got out on the town and pulled some harmless pranks.

Your family, however, had no idea where you were and basically freaked. They looked for you everywhere; and once you realized it, trying not to get caught became the game. In the middle of all the chaos you heard it. That one distinctive voice that makes your heart beat faster because you know you're gonna get it, but it's a really safe feeling at the same time. It's your Dad. He calls, you hear it, and you know you've been found. Somehow, you hear something in his voice that says things will be all right, despite what you have just done.

When we decide to run away from God, He still calls. How will you respond?

The Lord is in his Holy Temple; all the earth should be silent in his presence. > > > > > > > > > > > >

Chill for a little while.
God might be trying to tell you something.

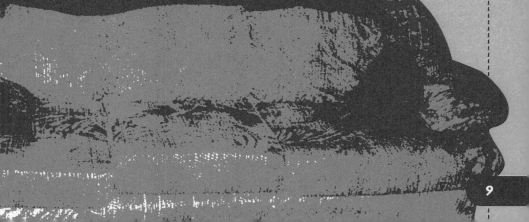

After he had sent them away, he went by himself up into the hills to pray. It was late, and Jesus was there alone. > > > > > > > > > > > > > > > > > > > > > > > >

The thought of being alone freaks you. You've got to have something going on all the time. Fight the fear! On the other side of it is God. The silence can't kill you. He wants to get you alone. Did you know that? No distractions. No other voices. Are you willing to risk it?

Find a spot. It might even be the same spot every time—that's cool, as long as you're alone. Maybe it's your room, your wheels, where you camp, anywhere. You just know that when you go there, it is a place where you have the ability to get away from it all and just think about what God wants you to think about, with no distractions. It isn't that He doesn't talk to you anywhere else, it's just that you *listen* better in that place.

Before you read again, go to that spot. Listen to what God wants you to know.

## >> Matthew 6:17-18

So when you give up eating, comb your hair and wash your face. Then people will not know that you are giving up eating, but your Father, whom you cannot see, will see you. Your Father sees what is done in secret, and he will reward you. > > > > >

When was the last time that you had a craving that you didn't give in to? Did you want a CD, clothes, maybe even a car? Picture this: You really want it, yet you deny yourself. And it's not because you don't have the money. It's just a decision you make. A decision to not buy anything new for one month. Now you're at the mall and your will is being tested. But you choose to deprive yourself of something so that you may accomplish something else.

That is the whole concept of fasting. It isn't something you brag about, letting the whole world know what you're doing. It's just between you and God. But what's the point? Well, every time you think about that thing you want—a Big Mac, the new Blink-182 CD, or that awesome sweater from Abercrombie—let it remind you of God. And listen to what he's telling you. Try it. Maybe for a meal, a day, or however long you want. Maybe even do it with a few friends and you guys can find out together what God is telling you through your fast.

11

## >> Philippians 4:4

It is the single greatest accomplishment of your life. You were snowboarding with your comrades, and you did the magical seven-twenty. Two complete revolutions in the air—very smooth. People around you gasped and cheered. You still can't really believe that you actually did it. Your partner on the slopes had the cam rolling and got the extreme footage for all to see. Now what? Celebration! You have just successfully completed a move you've been trying for years! It's great to be excited about it. Share the moment with as many people as are interested.

But let's imagine it again. This time you didn't make it. You know what? There is still plenty to celebrate in your life. Because it's not based on what you do, but on who you are. You are the kid of a King. A prince. A princess. And nothing you would do could ever change that. So win or lose, always celebrate the fact that you will inherit the kingdom one day.

Now, confess it to the Lord, the God of your ancestors. Do his will and separate yourselves from the people living around you. >>>>>>>>>>

## >> Ezra 10:11

Not only did you not expect it to happen, you didn't expect it to be so much fun. You really didn't want to go, but when he asked you out you were so surprised you just blurted out okay. Problem: You knew your best friend was *very* interested in him. If she knew you two went out she would be totally ticked. What a dilemma: your best friend or the guy. He is a really great guy, you've come to find out. On the other hand, she is your best friend.

You decide it is time to come clean, with both of them. First, you go to your best friend. You tell her the situation. She might even be okay with it. Or, she might not be okay with it, in which case you have to decide between the two. (I'd suggest your best friend in most cases; it's not likely that you'll end up marrying the guy.)

Next, you go to the guy. Tell him the deal. (If it's just to be friends, invite him to hang with your group this weekend.) DO NOT tell him that the reason you're saying all this is that your best friend digs him. That's her business to tell.

Now I would like to tell you that everything is going to work out perfectly, but I can't. What I can tell you is this: we have to be honest with each other. If we've screwed up, we've got to ask for forgiveness. First to God, then to anyone else involved.

> Do what you learned and received from me, what I told you, and what you saw me do. And the God who gives peace will be with you. >>>>>>>>

Do you really believe all this? You know what I'm asking. Do you really believe all that you read in the Bible? You would think the answer would be obvious since you are reading this book, but what about your life? If the Bible, Jesus, and the work of God really matter to you, does your life reflect it? Don't just say yes—think about how you live your life. Think about everything you did last weekend. Does it reflect your devotion to Jesus? If not, what do you need to change?

The Bible will guide your life; we know that is true. But you have to let it. You not only have to believe what it says, but it should also be evident in the way you live your life.

Come back to the Lord and say these words to him: "Take away all our sin and kindly receive us, and we will keep the promises we made to you." > > > > >

Why do we talk differently when we talk about God? You've heard it: when someone gets up at church to pray, and they start speaking in a different voice, saying words like "dearest Lord of all Creation" and "in supplication we beseech you to, blah blah blah." Christianese kicks in and the rest of the world goes, "What just happened?" Why do we do this? Do you think God is impressed with the way we talk all holy and all? Doubt it. He probably laughs with the rest of us.

Listen. Just talk to Him the same way you talk to your friends. Tell Him what's up. Don't feel like you need to change the way you talk in order for Him to appreciate it or get it. He understands you just fine. The problem is that we don't talk to Him enough. We probably spend more time talking to our animals than to Him. When you talk to Him about everything, you can't help but be yourself with Him. Tell Him what you love about Him, why you might be mad at Him. He already knows what you are going to say, so don't worry about hiding anything. If you're an online kind of person, then e-mail Him. Maybe you like to use the phone. Then unplug the handset and use it to say what you want. Just talk to Him. If you're an introvert, say it quietly in your heart. Just talk to Him.

Are you getting the point? Just talk to Him.

## >> 1 Timothy 1:12-14

It is easier to be mad than to forgive. Chances are, you can think of a person right now that you need to get right with. They

I thank Christ Jesus our Lord, who gave me strength, because he trusted me and gave me this work of serving him. In the past I spoke against Christ and persecuted him and did all kinds of things to hurt him. But God showed me mercy, because I did not know what I was doing. I did not believe. But the grace of our Lord was fully given to me, and with that grace came the faith and love that are in Christ Jesus. >>>>>>>>>>>>>>>>>>>>>

might have done something petty, like not calling you back. Or as major as abuse. But you are still called to forgive.

Why? Why would God ask you to forgive someone when they do something wrong, especially as awful as abuse or murder? Two reasons. One, we are asked to be more like Christ. And Christ came to earth to offer everyone forgiveness. Everyone. You want it, you gotta give it. Two, without forgiveness you will forever be a slave to the perpetrator. It might seem like the opposite, but until you get over it, they will own a piece of your heart.

Forgiveness might be the toughest road to take, but sometimes the hardest journey leads to the biggest treasure. Fight your right to be angry. And claim your right to forgive.

Can a person...change the color of his skin? Can a leopard change his spots? In the same way, Jerusalem, you cannot change and do good, because you are accustomed to doing evil. > > > > > > > > > >

Old habits die hard. At least the bad ones do. Of course, it's only a bad habit to the person it annoys. Take toilet seats. If you're a girl, you think the seat should be left down all the time. Your life is set in a "toilet-seat-down" mode. Guys, on the other hand, see no problem with leaving the seat up. This is their mode. Only they have moms and sisters constantly complaining about the position of the seat. So, who is wrong? It's an issue of personal convenience. Nothing is written in the Bible about toilet seat placement.

But what is written is to do to others what you would like them to do to you. In other words, don't make life harder on people. That's not your job, it's the enemy's. Life isn't about following the letter of the law—it's about loving other people and God. Do any of your "habits" bug someone else? Do you think you are tough enough to make a change, not because it's the law but just because you want to be able to love people?

Where in the world does God hang out? You ever wondered that? Does He prefer the diner or the movie theater? Or does He just prefer heaven and makes as few trips to earth as He possibly can?

You aren't alone in feeling like you can't find Him. Even great men of the Bible felt like God was a million miles away. Safe and sound in Heaven or someplace while they rotted away on earth. David was the total "where are you, God?" whiner. Check out Psalm 13. You aren't alone when you feel like you are. There are others who are feeling the exact same way. But here's the key. David had it. Even though He doesn't *feel* close, he had to *believe*, 'cuz that's what we are—*believers* that He is faithful and true. That He will "never leave us, nor forsake us." Even if it doesn't feel like it. So don't let your feelings lie to you; they'll try, but you know the truth. If you are unsure, then read some more of God's word. Learn from the lives of other lonely believers.

## >> Proverbs 1:5

Are you pretty much always right? Are you so sure that you are right that you won't listen to anyone else spout off their opinions at all? Maybe you are just so focused on what you believe that you can't find room to figure out why someone else would believe differently. If you are that focused, you might be coming across as narrow-minded, unwilling to at least try to understand someone else's point of view. Yuck! If this is you, I have a question you might not wanna hear. You ready?

Did you ever once consider that you might be wrong? Or even worse, that you might be the only one that doesn't know you're wrong. You won't lose your faith if you listen to a different opinion, even if it's someone who doesn't believe in God, or someone who does but in a totally different way than you. It won't mean you agree with them. But the deal is, if you want them to hear you out, you need to listen *first* and speak second. Don't pretend to know it all! There will always be someone who knows more. Just be willing to listen and slow to offer your opinions and answers.

From Paul, a servant of God and an apostle of Jesus Christ. I was sent to help the faith of God's chosen people and to help them know the truth that shows people how to serve God. That faith and that knowledge come from the hope for life forever, which God promised to us before time began. And God cannot lie. >>>>>>>>>>>>>>>>>>>

You have become so open-minded that you've forgotten what it is you stand for. You consider yourself a real free spirit, one who takes it all in and can become everything to everyone. After all, you don't want to appear narrow-minded. There are a couple of reasons for hiding behind the sham of "open-mindedness." First, you might still be searching for answers yourself. Second, it can be a convenient excuse to avoid finding true answers to hard questions, possibly concerning your faith. The problem is when people sense that you stand for nothing, they lose trust in you. People quit asking you for answers to issues in their life because your views change everyday. You have become so open-minded that your brains are starting to leak out of your head. But there is hope.

Everyone, deep down inside, has what we call a system of beliefs. It may not be worn on your shirtsleeve for all to see, but it is what you believe to be true. You'll hear people call it your "worldview." It's there inside, and you use it as a filter through which you see the world around you. Your worldview might be your truth, but is it God's truth?

## >> Luke 18:37

It is easily the weirdest predicament that you have ever been caught in. Your biology teacher claims that, through his class, you have seen evidence that supports the Theory of Evolution. You must buy into the theory in order to get a good grade, and save yourself from being ragged on by your friends. So what do you do? You have heard your teacher's argument, and on paper he can make a pretty good case. But it goes against everything that you have been brought up to believe and know to be true in your heart.

As your teacher proceeds with the discussion, he asks if anyone in the class has a different idea. Now that big lump in the back of your throat shows up. You really want to make your case for Creation, but you don't know enough to argue with a teacher. But what the heck. Here goes. When you're done the teacher shoots you down, line by line. He makes you look like a total dork. You are speechless. Your friends who know your convictions are proud of you. God is proud of you. It doesn't matter if you won or lost. You stood up, and that's what rocks.

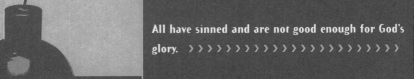

## >> Romans 3:23

Sin. We hear the word thrown around all the time. "Don't do that, it's a sin," or "you're sinning," maybe even "you're letting sin have it's way with you." We throw the term around, but what does it really mean? There are a ton of definitions rolling around, and it just starts to seem like a bunch of clichés. But what does sin really mean? It has to mean something because we are all guilty of it. Try this. Messing up. Being stupid. Getting it wrong. Ever done any of that? My dad never minds me failing, but no way would he approve of me not trying. Fear of messing up or getting it wrong is no excuse for not trying. I know I'll never be to the point where I'm sin-free, but that doesn't mean I should give up tryin' to be.

If you have one particularly gnarly sin, you're gonna have to take it one day at a time. God really is honored by our moves toward a tighter relationship with Him. That means trying to get rid of the sin stuff in our life.

"The people who live now are living in a sinful and evil time. If people are ashamed of me and my teaching, the Son of Man will be ashamed of them when he comes with his Father's glory and with the holy angels." >>>>>>>>>>>>>>>>>>>>>

It is a prayer that we pray only sometimes, and often we hope that God won't give us what we ask for. I'm talking about boldness in your faith. It is much easier to hide behind your shyness than to go out and boldly proclaim the truth about Jesus. It's much easier to say nothing than to tell a friend we don't like it when they get angry and yell "Jesus Christ." It's a weird concept, but we deny God when we don't say anything about Him. We need to constantly pray for boldness with our faith.

*God, I confess that I've been a jerk for not sticking up for You. I know that You can take care of Yourself, but it still isn't right. Help me to be tough when I need to talk about who You are and what You're up to in my life. I don't want You to be just another part of my life; I want You to be every part of my life. Help me talk freely, especially when I don't know exactly what to say.*

## >> Galatians 6:9

You get so tired of constantly being told no. It isn't from your 'rents, it's your friends! They keep giving you the big negative sign when you ask them to come to youth group stuff with you. You know they would like it if they would just give it a chance. But because it is being put on by a church or ministry, they avoid it like the plague. It would be so much easier to give up and completely focus on yourself and what you get out of the ministry. Problem is that the kingdom of God isn't built by people who give up. There comes a time when you need to ask God for some perseverance.

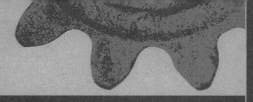

## >> Proverbs 23:16

You know you didn't work as hard on the project as you should have. You didn't work hard at all! Usually you get into a class project and overachieve, but this time was different. Too many other things to do and for some reason your heart just wasn't into this one. You figure it won't matter. You have always pulled decent grades. You aren't totally concerned. Then you see your grade, and it bites. A big red "see me after class" is written across the top of the page. Duh, duh, duh, duuuuuh!!!!

You go and talk with the teacher, and he wants to know what's up. He's concerned because "This isn't like you." Then the excuses start rollin'. You have a job, your parents give you too many chores, and on and on.

Stop! Shut up. How about just tellin' the truth? Yeah, you have a lot on your plate, but you thought you could slide by on your good rep. Your heart just wasn't in it, and you honestly don't know why. Hey, that's okay. Sometimes that's the way it is. But don't lie. Be honest and responsible. People will trust you more if you consistently level with 'em.

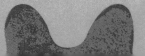

Pray in the Spirit at all times with all kinds of prayers, asking for everything you need. To do this you must always be ready and never give up. Always pray for all God's people. >>>>>>>>>>>>

People say prayer is so simple, but it sure doesn't seem like it. Sometimes it feels like God is a million miles away. What do your little problems have to do with His running the universe? And sometimes your problems are so gross you would just rather not talk about them with the Creator of the universe.

"My Lord God, I have no idea where I am going. I do not see the road ahead of me. I cannot know for certain where it will end. Nor do I really know myself, and the fact that I think that I am following Your will does not mean that I am actually doing so. But I believe that the desire to please You does in fact please You. And I hope I have that desire in all that I am doing. I hope that I will never do anything apart from that desire. I will not fear, for you are ever with me, and you will never leave me to face my perils alone." Thomas Merton prayed that in his book *On Solitude*. Try it out.

Joshua also put twelve rocks in the middle of the Jordan River where the priests had stood while carrying the Ark of the Agreement. These rocks are still there today. > > > > > > > > > > > > > > > > > > > >

The place may not be important, but the symbol is. We have all done some majorly amazing things in our lives that are worth remembering. It might be when you finally let God be God in your life. Or maybe it's the place where you decided you wanted to take the plunge—be baptized. Or ever think, "Wow, God totally heard me on that and look how it turned out. My prayer was answered with a big fat yes?" Then find a symbol to remind you of how awesome He is. Remembering the major stuff in your life is way important. It helps you look back and see all the stuff that God has done. After crossing the Jordan to dry ground, Joshua picked up twelve stones to be his symbol of God doing that awesome miracle. Now your symbols don't have to be stones, but what kinda stuff can you use? A photo of the event, a candle that was burned, a ticket stub—anything that reminds you of the moment. Put it in a place where you will see it all the time. And every time you look at it, it will remind you that God does work in your life.

Praise his glorious name forever. Let his glory fill the whole world. Amen and amen. >>>>>>>

Just praise God today. Sing. Paint. Write. Play. Praise Him.

Another man said, "I will follow you, Lord, but first let me go and say good-bye to my family." Jesus said, "Anyone who begins to plow a field but keeps looking back is of no use in the kingdom of God." > > > >

Risk. It's a scary thing. You want to write this note—would they think you were a dork? You want to plan a surprise party for your best friend's birthday, but what if it turns out lame? Again, dork! You'd like to be in the play; it looks fun, but, argh, auditions! It's called risk: doing something that you want to do but aren't sure how you'll look if you do. But would you rather spend your life in caution mode? Afraid to step out and risk the dreaded defeat? Have a nice life. Listen, you'll get nowhere in life if you aren't willing to risk. You can think and dream all you want, but until you do something, it will stay a dream.

You really want to share your amazing relationship with Jesus with this friend. What's stoppin' ya? Fear of what she might think? You can play it through in your head a zillion times with a zillion different possibilities, and all of them could be wrong. You'll never know how it will go until you actually do it. A life without risk is no life at all. You willing to live like that? Bored out of your gourd? Or do you want to risk it all? Remember, it's not a risk if there is no possibility of failure. Do you dare?

Don't fear, little flock, because your Father wants to give you the kingdom. >>>>>>>>>>>>>>>>>>

Remember how scared you used to get when you and your gang would sit in the dark and tell creepy stories late at night? Sleep? After that? You've got to be kidding. Finally some "coward" would turn on the light and all the other "cowards" would breathe a sigh of relief. You know they all wanted the light on too.

Today, your fears might be entirely different, but they have something in common with those creepy nights. They are built up in your mind worse than actual reality. What do you fear? Failing in school, loneliness, no crush, or rejection? All of these are valid fears that you've probably exaggerated in your mind.

So what do you do? Let's initiate a counter-attack. Check it out. If you're freaked about failing school, study for thirty more minutes today, and then forget about it. Afraid of being lonely? Then spend a little more time this week with a bud. If you don't like the feeling of rejection (and who does?) then take time with the people you meet. Talk to them and make sure they don't feel rejected by you. Fear has no power over you. Stop it in its tracks. "NO! You have no power over me. I will do all I can through Christ to conquer what is real and not be consumed by what isn't."

So when you give to the poor, don't let anyone know what you are doing. > > > > > > > > > > > > > > > >

Buy your mom flowers, clean your room without being asked, drop an anonymous dinner gift certificate to your youth pastor, or clean toilets at the local shelter. Do it, and don't get caught. Don't let anyone else know what you did. Keeping the secret is the goal. See if you can give without ever being found out. We give out of love, not because of what we get back.

>> Luke 12:22-23

Jesus said to his followers, "So I tell you, don't worry about the food you need to live, or about the clothes you need for your body. Life is more than food, and the body is more than clothes. > > > >

Brand names. For or against? Does it make sense to wear anything less than Tommy, American Eagle, A&F? If it isn't name brand, there's no way that you'd be caught dead in it. Ever change your outfit eight times before school, piles of clothes strewn all over the room, looking for the perfect ensemble? Or have you perfected the messy look? It takes forty-five minutes but it's hard to be beautiful. A person's gotta work at the perfect image. Mom, of course, thinks you dress like a slob. "Pull those pants up!" Dad thinks you look "inappropriate." But give up the look you've worked so hard on? No way José. Sometimes you just have to put your foot down—you just won't go if you can't wear what you want. The parentals just don't get it.

News flash. Your image shouldn't be wrapped up in threads. It's got to come from inside. Stressing over the right clothes might say a little bit about where your priorities are. Eeek! That's scary. Where are yours?

A lazy person will end up poor, but a hard worker will become rich. > > > > > > > > > > > > > > > > > > > >

Are you lazy? At least according to your parents? You are if this sounds familiar: "All you do is play video games," or "Don't you ever get off the phone?"

You don't see anything wrong with entertaining yourself, but it makes your parents nutso. They just don't see the value. RPGs or chatting on the phone aren't bad—when you ignore the 'rents to do it, you've got a prob.

So what's the trick? How do you do what you love without being a lazy fool? Consider the future. Find out what you love and figure out how to make something productive out of it. What you love to do for fun could lead you to what you want to be. You like sports? Maybe you have a future in sports journalism. Check out the subject. You dig watching movies? Maybe you should look into writing movie reviews for the local paper. Don't get caught in the trap of doing nothing. Be productive no matter what you are doing, from playing video games to talking on the phone. What does God want you to do with your passions?

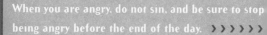

> When you are angry, do not sin, and be sure to stop being angry before the end of the day. >>>>>>

Try this: Buy a tube of toothpaste and squeeze it out onto a sheet of paper. Now take a knife and try to get all of the toothpaste back into the tube. No matter how hard you try or how long you work at it, you can't get it all back in. You can scrape all you want, but there ain't no way to do it. What's done is done, there's no going back to the way it was.

The same thing happens when you're really ticked off. It's like leftover toothpaste. You say something mean, take a swing at someone, smash something up, rip pages out of your book, drive like a maniac. Problem is, once you've flipped out on someone, you can't take back your actions. Sure, you can be forgiven, but you can never ever take them back, no matter how hard you try.

Is it really worth it? Anger isn't wrong. It's what you do with it that is right or wrong. Control is an amazing thing. You can take control of your anger before it takes control of you. Slow down, take a deep breath, and think. I know that's hard, but do you want to win or lose? The winner is the one who has control of his or her emotions. Think about what makes you angry. Now figure out how to *respond* to it; don't *react*, 'cuz that's where you lose.

>> Galatians 6:7

Do not be deceived. God is not mocked: for whatever a man sows, that he will also reap. >>>>>>>>

You raced home today. *Sports Illustrated*'s swimsuit issue is in your mailbox, and you've got to make sure you get it out before your mom gets home from work. The guys will all be talking about it tomorrow. Blaaazing! There it is. Wow! How easy is that? You get up to your room and flip it open; your fantasies start to come to life. You imagine things you'd "never do in real life." And hey, you aren't hurting anyone, so why not? If you weren't supposed to see this stuff, it wouldn't be in a sports magazine, right? Most of your friends would agree. But suddenly, this one magazine isn't enough. You flip on the computer and type in the address to that site you heard about in the locker room where the girls are actually naked.

So what's next? A prostitute? A real live interaction? Sound appalling? You'd never ever do something that creepy? Well, news flash, you already have. "Anyone who looks at a woman lustfully has already committed adultery with her in his heart."

Realize, and realize it now, that what you sit around thinking about you've already done as far as Jesus is concerned. Don't believe in pre-marital sex? Then why are you committing it in your mind? Don't be deceived—God will not be mocked.

## >> Daniel 2:21b

Election season. Your history teacher is acting like a total dork, he's so into it. But what are you going to do? Everyone keeps telling you it's your "duty as a citizen" to go vote. Geez. You don't even care about politics—they're all liars and cheats anyway, right?

Well, after some soul searching you decide that you want your voice to count for something, so you're gonna go do it. But now you've got a new crisis. Who are you gonna vote for? Your parents are Republicans and say, "You have to vote for the Republican candidate"—no matter who it is. You've seen lots of posters around town for this other guy. And that independent candidate is really cute. (Hint: that's not the way to decide.) Get online and read about 'em, watch a debate or two on TV, figure out what they believe in and then vote. God gave you a brain—use it! You've got a chance to make a difference here.

One time when Jesus was praying alone, his followers were with him, and he asked them, "Who do the people say I am?" They answered, "Some say you are John the Baptist. Others say you are Elijah. And others say you are one of the prophets from long ago who has come back to life." Then Jesus asked, "But who do you say I am?" > > > > > > > >

I love baseball. It's the coolest game to watch. I know some people might think it's slow, but I dig it. I am totally into baseball history. One of my favorite stories is Babe Ruth's called shot. This is how it goes: New York was playing Chicago. Babe was at the plate. He pointed out to the center field bleachers and took his stance. He had to dodge a couple that were aimed more at his head than the strike zone. But the next time he got a chance to swing at a pitch, he hit the ball to the exact spot he had pointed. Now many historians differ as to whether this *really* happened. Of course Chicago fans say it never happened, and New York fans will assure you it did. I am not gonna argue one side or the other, but wouldn't it be great if it were true? However the only way to get to the truth is to investigate the historic evidence.

The same thing happens with Jesus. One side says He never lived, the other says He did. Tons don't believe He was resurrected, others say He was. What do you say? Don't just take your parents' word for it or anybody else's. Go to your local library or search the Internet for proof of His life and the stuff He did. It's out there. Find out on your own.

Praise the Lord, all nations on earth. Praise the Lord's glory and power; praise the glory of the Lord's name. Bring an offering and come to him. Worship the Lord because he is holy. >>>>>>>>>>>>>>>>>>>

So if you can't sing, can you still worship? I mean what if your voice totally bites, and the guy next to you moves away so you won't distract him. Does it distract you so you feel like you can't even worship? It's just not your thing? Do you ever wish there were another option? I mean singing can't be the only way, can it? Heck no! There are tons more. Love to draw? Next time you are into worship, break out your pens and sketch somethin' for Him. Let Him speak through your pen onto the paper. At home, break out your little sis's clay and sculpt something for Him. Write a poem. Do whatever you feel you're good at, only do it in response to the Creator who pulses in your heart. If worship was just singing, there would only be a select few who would be able to give God all that oozes out of their heart. Use all of your talents as an offering to Him. He totally digs it.

I have prayed that you will not lose your faith! Help your brothers be stronger when you come back to me. >>>>>>>>>>>>>>>>>>>>>>>

Do you ever wonder what or how you should pray for your friends? Some friends are easy to pray for, but others seem to have their life together. Guess what: all your friends have junk in their lives that you don't know anything about. When you talk to God for someone else, you are "interceding" for them to God. That is where the term "intercessory prayer" comes from. A simple prayer you can always pray for your friends is that they will experience God more and more.

Try this: *God, I admit that I don't know how to pray for _____, but I know that You want me to. So I pray that Your relationship with them would be totally tight. Let them feel Your presence closer than their skin. Let them crave time with You, and most of all let them know deep, deep down how much You totally love them. You rock!*

## »» 1 Samuel 15:28

It's your turn. Dad always takes one of you on his yearly triporama to Australia, and it's your turn. You can hardly wait. You are going "down under," and you have major plans brewin' in your brain. Snorkeling, shopping, beach bumming, and kangaroo racing are all on the agenda. As the trip gets closer, you haven't heard a thing from Dad about going. You finally ask him what's up. "Oops, didn't I tell you?" he asks. "I've decided to take your uncle and your cousin." Your favorite cousin! Well, used to be your favorite cousin. It is totally unfair that he gets to go and you don't! It's over. You'll never see or talk to Dad or your uncle or cousin again.

This must be how Jonathan felt. He should have been the king of Israel, but Dad had other plans. Jonathan was a godly man, but he would not rule the kingdom. David would. Yet instead of getting really ticked off, Jonathan did the unthinkable. He became best buds with David and did everything he could to protect him. And it was genuine—not just so he could get what he wanted now that David was king.

You can't always choose what happens to you—life ain't fair. But you can choose how you will respond to those things. Take Jonathan's lead. Get over yourself and find out what God wants you to do next.

## >> Luke 15:1-2

The tax collectors and sinners all came to listen to Jesus. But the Pharisees and the teachers of the law began to complain: "Look, this man welcomes sinners and even eats with them." >>>>>>>>>

What a trip! You would have never believed it. It can't be true. She is so popular. She was voted prettiest in the sophomore class. All the guys totally dig her. How could she be gay? She's not your best friend, but you've been in church together since kindergarten. How did you miss it? Lots of people have started making fun of her behind her back. And to be honest, you're not quite sure what to say to her anymore. Just remember that the "greatest commandment" is to love your neighbor. Don't treat her like she has the plague. Right now, the issue is love and it might be your reputation on the line. She needs a good friend to talk to because this is tough stuff she is going through. Who do you want to be like, the Pharisees or Jesus? The choice is yours.

But when the Holy Spirit comes to you, you will receive power. You will be my witnesses—in Jerusalem, in all of Judea, in Samaria, and in every part of the world. >>>>>>>>>>>>>>>>>

Not today. You're gonna be late for school. You have no time today. "I can't stop for this accident, Lord," you say. "The people behind me can stop." You gotta go. But you were the one who saw it happen. Dang it! You know you gotta stop. Ten minutes later, the police arrive and start asking questions. When they get to you, you tell them the events of the accident as you saw them. Nothing but the facts. You don't place blame anywhere, you just tell the story as you saw it. Nothing less, nothing more and not too difficult.

The same could and should be true when you tell people about Jesus. He never told us to go out and make it harder than it ought to be. He told us to be His witnesses, to tell people what we have seen and what we know to be true about Him. Don't feel weird or tongue-tied, just tell your story the best way that you know how.

The Lord sees everything you do, and he watches where you go. An evil man will be caught in his wicked ways; the ropes of his sins will tie him up. He will die because he does not control himself, and he will be held captive by his foolishness. >>

If you could get away with a lie would you try? Come on, 'fess up. What if it were the best choice you could come up with? And besides, it could save your hide. Mom and Dad will never know. As you backed their car out of the parking spot at school you smacked the one next to you. Screetch! The cars were swapping paint. So now what? No one saw you, so what were you going to do, sit there and wait? How about jet? I mean, what else can you do? If you hang around to tell the truth, you'll never drive again. Why not take the easy way out? When you get home you tell your dad the car was like that when you got out of class. Totally ticked, your dad calls the school and goes off on security. He can't believe the jerk didn't leave a note on your car! Now you are really freaked. What if the owner of the other car calls the school and says the same thing? You'll be dead meat. Better start working on another lie . . .

There is a major epidemic running through our culture today, and it is called lying. Why do people do it? To impress, to avoid trouble, or just because they can't think of something to say. What was the last lie you told? You might even have gotten away with it, but God knows. Most of the time lies don't just end. You have to tell bigger lies to cover up the first one. Don't get caught in the trap.

## >> 2 Kings 2:23-24

From there Elisha went up to Bethel. On the way some boys came out of the city and made fun of him. They said to him, "Go up too, you baldhead! Go up too, you baldhead!" Elisha turned around, looked at them, and put a curse on them in the name of the Lord. Then two mother bears came out of the woods and tore forty-two of the boys to pieces. 〉 〉 〉 〉 〉

Does this small account from the life of Elisha make you think about how you treat people? Plain and simple, be careful who you dis' because you never know what they might do to get back at you! Okay, I doubt bears will come out of the woods and eat you, but here's the point: We should always be aware of people's feelings when we talk to them, especially people we don't know very well, 'cause we don't know exactly how they will take what we say. What might be funny to you might not be funny to them. You don't know what their history is. Be careful how you tease people. It's easy to take teasing too far. You usually don't mean anything by it, but the damage is done. The results of teasing someone who does not want to be teased can be disastrous.

## >> Ezra 9:6

I prayed, "My God, I am too ashamed and embarrassed to lift up my face to you, my God, because our sins are so many. They are higher than our heads. Our guilt even reaches up to the sky. > > > > > > > > > >

How in the world did this happen? You have never felt so awful in your whole life. It will most definitely take the rest of your life to get over it. Maybe you cheated on a test or college entrance exam. Or you and your boyfriend got going and just couldn't stop. Maybe you've stolen a car to prove to the guys that you're cool enough. Did you blow up on your parents and tell them that you hate them? Whatever it is, it is so big that you can hardly believe you did it. Now you're living with major baggage—guilt, shame. It's getting so bad that you're starting to think you can never face God again. You know He forgives, but how can He forgive you? You can't even forgive yourself!

Well, it's time to be free. Own up to your sin and move on. How do you move on? Do whatever you have to do to make right—it won't be easy, but do it. Tell God about it and get His help moving on. Know that God's love for you is always there.

## >> Mark 3:14

You wouldn't be causing trouble or anything, would you? Hangin' with all your buds? Up to no good? Well, maybe that's what the 'rents think. But it totally isn't that. It's just hangin', doing nothing at all. In fact, to an outsider it might even seem boring. Sittin' on a street corner and watching cars go by. Going over to someone's house. Loitering at the bowling alley. Your parents are suspicious, but there is really nothing wrong with what you're doing.

Take a look at the life of Jesus. When He called the twelve disciples to follow Him, what was the first thing on His agenda? Check out Mark 3:14. He wanted them to be with Him. To do what? A little preaching and a little deliverance, but first and foremost it was to hang together. Even today Jesus still wants to hang out with those He loves. But for some reason, many people whom He loves don't want to hang with Him. Go hang out with Jesus for a while.

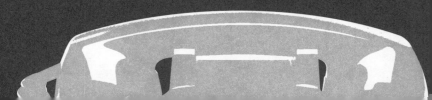

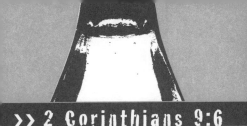

## >> 2 Corinthians 9:6

The day you dread is here. Once a year your mom decides that it is time to try a new church for a Sunday. She wants to make sure she really likes the one you go to now.

So you get there, find a seat, sit down, and begin to sing a bunch of songs you've never heard before. Right now you would rather be at the dentist having cavities filled. Suddenly you notice this guy sitting in front of you. He used to go to your Jr. High, but now he goes to the High School across town. During the time when you're supposed to say good morning to the person next to you, you talk with him, and it blows you away. He really has a deep love for God and people. In Jr. High you would have never guessed he would end up in church, so you never invited him. Now someone else has, and here he is. You start to think through how many other people you've never told that you know God, let alone love Him. What can you change about this in the future?

## >> Proverbs 3:21

Her mom is the coolest woman you have ever met. She is a mom who
gets teenagers without trying to be one. Her kids can stay out as long as
they want on weekends and don't even have to call to tell where they
are going. "If only my parents could be like that," you think. To have a
mom that is so secure, so free-thinking, and so fun to be around—that is
the family you wanna be in.

One weekend your friend has a party, and naturally you are invited.
Her mom is there, and you notice something different about her. She
doesn't seem to be quite all together. When you're talking to her, she
offers you some pot. At first you think, "What harm could it do? There
are a lot of people who do it, and they seem to be okay." And you have
always been curious to know what the big deal is about marijuana. As
she passes you the joint, you notice her eyes are really glazed, and she
just starts giggling uncontrollably. Suddenly she doesn't seem to be so
cool. In fact, she doesn't seem to be the same person anymore. That's the
reality. If you use pot, you won't be the same person anymore either.

That's it, you've had it! You no longer want to be a part of this family. As far as you're concerned, it isn't even a family. In a real family, everyone is treated equally, right? Well, that's what you think. And in this family your brother's girlfriend gets treated better than you do! She got to borrow your parents' car when you really needed it. Never mind that you never told anyone you needed the car. You just assumed it would be yours. Well that's it, no more! You are leaving. You pack up some things and decide to go live with a friend. He has his own apartment, and you figure you can crash with him.

After sleeping on his old, uncomfortable couch for two nights, you are really missing your old bed. Lying there, you realize that your anger got the best of you, and you might have made a bad choice. The only way out is to suck it up and talk to your parents, like you should have done in the first place. When you are ticked off, don't let the anger set in and control you. Talk to your parents. Let them know why you're frustrated. And make sure you take time to listen to them.

. . . and gave thanks for it. Then he broke the bread and said, "This is my body; it is for you. Do this to remember me." >>>>>>>>>>>>>

It's that awesome time of the year when it just starts to turn into fall—it's still warm outside but cool at the same time. Life is just perfect right now. But then suddenly the news arrives. There was a school shooting just across town. You are stunned. Totally numb. Not in this city, not this close. You actually might know some of the students who were killed. You can't believe it's actually happened; you're kinda in denial. A few weeks and months later the cops have figured it all out, and a memorial is built to remember the kids from your youth group who died. Every year, on the anniversary of the tragedy, people from all over bring flowers to the school. It's a small sign of remembering and a call for it to never happen again. A way to honor those who lost their lives.

The next time you have a chance to take part in communion, put it into perspective. It's a way of remembering Someone who gave His life, in the most heinous way possible. It is good to remember.

**But when Philip told them the Good News about the kingdom of God and the power of Jesus Christ, men and women believed Philip and were baptized.**

> > > > > > > > > > > > > > > > > > > > > > > > > > >

It is one of your most prized possessions. You love it more than your dog and skateboard put together. It's your state championship ring that you won with the golf team last year. It is gold with a cool diamond-looking rock in the middle. You wear it with pride. Everyone who sees the ring totally digs it and asks you how you got it. You love telling the story of how you went from fourth place to first in the last day of the tournament, securing the championship. Okay, you had to pay for the ring yourself, a slight drawback. But no one except you got one. It's a symbol that says something about you and what you've done.

Have you ever wondered about baptism? In every account in the Book of Acts, baptism is linked with belief. People *believed* in the good news of Jesus and *then* were baptized. It's an outward symbol of an inward belief. Be baptized with pride! Allow everyone to see your outward expression of your inward love for God.

But you, man of God, run away from all those things. Instead, live in the right way, serve God, have faith, love, patience, and gentleness. > > > >

You're sitting peacefully in your favorite bathroom stall, mindin' your own business when suddenly you hear a bunch of voices. Slowly, you recognize them. It's your gang. So you start eavesdropping. After all, you can't really help it. The person they are talking about must be a real gem 'cuz you hear things like "liar," "cheat," "dirtbag," and "freak." Wow, this is getting good. You lift your feet up to make sure that they don't notice someone is in the stall and stop the conversation. They keep going and it gets even more harsh. Then it happens. A blow from out of nowhere hits you right between the eyes. They're talking about you. Your eyes start to well up. You never, ever dreamed that people you considered friends would dis' you so harshly.

Look at what Paul says about Timothy in this verse: "You, man of God." Wouldn't it be great if people said things like that about you? How do you think your friends talk about you when you're not around? Be honest. What does that tell you?

I have noticed that people who plow evil and plant trouble harvest it. >>>>>>>>>>>>>>>>>

They are the best group to hang out with. Every time you get together you know something outrageous is going to happen. Then Keith starts hanging out with you guys and things take a twist. Keith doesn't want to just have fun. He wants to cause trouble. Destruction is the name of the game to him, and the more trouble you can cause without getting caught, the more fun the game is to him. He is a nice guy, but he wants to take everything to the extreme.

One night Keith suggests that you go behind a local store and set the back wall on fire, then sit back and time how long it takes the fire department to get there. Admit it, you're a coward. You like to have fun, pull a few pranks, but this is way more than you bargained for. You try to decline, while still looking cool. You suggest that it's not such a good idea. But Keith starts laying on a guilt trip in front of everybody, telling you he knew you couldn't handle something that wild.

They are just words, that's it. You know that destroying what isn't yours is not "fun," it's vandalism. You walk away. Keith proceeds and gets caught. You are so glad you didn't do something that stupid. As for Keith, he's facing the consequences. He has a hard road ahead of him.

## >> Job 42:7

After the Lord had said these things to Job, he said to Eliphaz the Temanite, "I am angry with you and your two friends, because you have not said what is right about me, as my servant Job did." >>>>>

What do you say about God? The assumption is that you know Him, since you are reading this book right now. Do you talk about Him in the right way? Are the things you say about Him true? Maybe you don't know the right way to speak about God. Have you ever found yourself telling your friends that "God helps those who help themselves?" I hate to break it to you, but that isn't in the Bible. So think about it. You might not be speaking what is right about God.

What do you do about it? Read the Bible and learn more about Him. He wants you to know Him better so you can talk about Him more often and more truthfully. We sometimes talk so much about God's love that we forget His justice; so much about His mercy that we fail to respect His power. Love God, yes. But make sure you know the One you love.

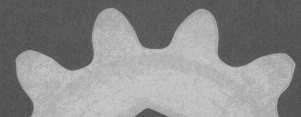

He saved us because of his mercy. It was not because of good deeds we did to be right with him. He saved us through the washing that made us new people through the Holy Spirit. > > > > > > > > > >

Amazing grace how sweet the sound that saved a wretch like me.
I once was lost, but now am found, was blind but now I see.

T'was grace that taught my heart to fear, and grace my fears relieved.
How precious did that grace appear, the hour I first believed.

Through many dangers, toils, and snares, I have already come;
'Tis grace hath brought me safe thus far, and grace will lead my home.

When we've been there ten thousand years, bright shining as the sun,
We've no less days to sing God's praise than when we've first begun.

John Newton 1725–1807

Jesus answered, "I am the way, and the truth, and the life. The only way to the Father is through me."
>>>>>>>>>>>>>>>>>>>>>>>>>>>>>>>

Really good people believe "it." Even a lot of Christians believe "it." But for some reason, you have trouble swallowing "it." You have been sitting in your religious philosophy class, listening to the various things people believe about a relationship with God and going to heaven. Some of these people have gone to church with you for years and they are buying into "it."

What is "it"? "It" is the belief that all roads lead to heaven. The notion that everyone, if they lead a good life and do more good things than bad things, will end up in heaven. But Jesus said that there is no way to the Father except through Him. A lot of religions teach excellent principles for living. Principles based on loving people, the earth, and God. That's great, but they leave one detail out. They don't know what to do with Jesus. The funny thing is most people agree with the principles that Jesus taught, with one big exception. That He is the only way to God. If He didn't mean it, why would He say it? Jesus said He is the only way because it is true. Don't let the people you care about be confused by "it."

Whoever forgives someone's sin makes a friend, but gossiping about the sin breaks up friendships.

>>>>>>>>>>>>>>>>>>>>>>>>>>>>>>>

You can't believe she did that! It's been a year and she has apologized several times. In fact, she apologizes every time you bring it up, but you still can't get over the fact that she made that mistake. She turned her back on God and her friends for a semester of drinking, partying, and sex. We all bite it from time to time; that's part of being human. As Christians, we have the luxury to realize that we aren't perfect. We don't encourage or condone mistakes, but we can expect that they will happen. And when they do, it is our honor as Christians to show each other the love Christ showed us by forgiving and forgetting. Don't keep score of the screw-ups and shortcomings of your friends. Do you want them to keep score on you?

## >> Acts 4:20

This might sound rebellious, but I'm saying it anyway: "Don't shut up." If you have good news to talk about, such as what you have seen God do in your life and the lives of your friends, tell people about it! As Christians, we are much too quiet. We have a great story to tell, but we tend to sit on it. Why is that? Are we scared? Embarrassed? Don't know what to say?

What keeps you quiet? Now, maybe you are the type of person that tells everyone about the work God is doing in your life. That's great, but don't go too far with it. Don't be annoying or all judgmental. But don't shut up, either! Find new ways to talk about God. Look for interesting ways to bring up what Jesus is doing in your life. Talk about it, don't stuff it and go through life with no one knowing how much God means to you. Force yourself to be told to shut up about God.

This is my prayer for you: that your love will grow more and more; that you will have knowledge and understanding with your love; that you will see the difference between good and bad and will choose the good; that you will be pure and without wrong for the coming of Christ . . . > > > > > > > > > > > >

No one wants to date her anymore and you can't figure out why. She's hot, smart, nice, and tons o' fun. You finally get the nerve to ask her out and when you do she immediately says yes. Wow!

You tell your buddies and they all look at you funny and give you a "haven't-you-heard?" laugh. Nobody wants to go out with her because she got "knocked up" by her last boyfriend. He broke up with her, saying he wasn't ready for kids. She felt totally freaked and trapped, so she had an abortion. Not many people knew at the time, but now the news is out. She has become really involved in church, so people are real quick to throw the "hypocrite" label on her. It isn't fair. In fact, in some way we are all hypocrites because we are all sinners. Everyone deals with sin issues. Some are more obvious than others, but they're all there.

How are you going to react, now that you know the whole story? Read the passage again and think about who you know that needs a little lovin'. Reach out to them, and let God work through you. Do the right thing.

Look around me and see. No one cares about me.
I have no place of safety; no one cares if I live.
> > > > > > > > > > > > > > > > > > > > > > > > > > > > > >

Have you ever felt like David did when he wrote this psalm? Lonely?
Depressed? You might have tons of friends. You might even be
surrounded by people all the time, but inside it really doesn't matter—
you're still lonely. Overwhelmed with loneliness.

Answer this. What do you think other people are thinking about
you? Do you think no one really cares? When David wrote this psalm
he was pretty discouraged, hiding in a cave, and fearing for his life.
Sure he was totally all alone. But after he whined for a while, he got
down to the truth that the Lord would take care of him.

If you feel as if no one really cares, try something different. Commit
yourself to some positive thinking. Start each day by believing that
everyone you come into contact with is genuinely excited to see you.
And be excited to see them too. Don't just try it once. Commit to it for
several days, even weeks. You will see that people do care about you
and are glad to have you around. Those feelings of loneliness should
soon disappear.

It is not fancy hair, gold jewelry, or fine clothes that should make you beautiful. No, your beauty should come from within you—the beauty of a gentle and quiet spirit that will never be destroyed and is very precious to God. >>>>>>>>>>>>>>>>>>>>

You have been getting ready all day long. This is going to be the night of your life. You waited a long time for him to ask you out, and now the big day is here. It's not just a date. It's an event.

Hair, teeth, fingernails, toenails, jewelry, and clothes all have to be perfect, and so far they are. The big moment is here. He's at the door. You open the door, and just then your little brother notices a string, pulls it, and rips your blouse. Now what? You ask your date to wait while you change into a different outfit. Good thing you had that back up outfit planned out! You feel like you look good again, and head out the door to the car. Suddenly the automatic sprinklers kick on. As you try to escape the water, you slip in some dog poo. The perfect date is turning into a perfect disaster. Sound familiar? Try, if you can, to laugh it off. Your date probably will, and you know why? Because it's funny! Looking good isn't the most important thing. It's how you handle uncontrollable circumstances that counts. Looks will fade someday, but your personality doesn't have to!

Then the LORD made the donkey talk, and she said to Balaam, "What have I done to make you hit me three times?" Balaam answered the donkey, "You have made me look foolish! I wish I had a sword in my hand! I would kill you right now!" >>>>

I remember the first time I read this verse. I was at church, and I laughed out loud so hard that I almost peed in my pants. I think my brother showed it to me, and it was in some old translation of the Bible, so it said "ass" instead of "donkey." I couldn't quit laughing. I thought it was hysterical to read in the Bible that God "opened the mouth of the ass."

You know, it's okay to laugh, because it's funny. "Ass" is a dirty word, and here I was reading it in the Bible. Actually, it was my mom's Bible, which made it so much funnier.

It's okay to laugh. God didn't make us to be serious all the time. There are things in this world that are funny, and we *should* laugh at them. Like yourself, sometimes you just have to laugh at yourself. Have a good laugh once in a while. It does the soul good. Different situations are funny to different people, so go nuts when something is funny to you. Laugh a lot, and always laugh at the stupid things you do.

> But you should do this: "If your enemy is hungry,
> feed him; if he is thirsty, give him a drink. Doing
> this will be like pouring burning coals on his head."

## >> Romans 12:20

Do you have an enemy? Someone who abused you? Tricked you? Stole from you? Dissed you? An enemy. Someone not on your side. Out to get you. What are ya supposed to do with them? Check it out: Love them.

What?!? Yep, you are supposed to treat them like someone who is on your side. How the heck do you do that? The easy answer is to treat them the same way you treat those people you care about. But it really isn't that simple when you're dealing with people that you can't stand, and who can't stand you in return.

So how do you love a jerk? Let's break it down. Be nice to them. That's really all it means. Be nice. They won't expect it. Think about it. It's really hard to be mean to someone who is being nice to you, because it makes you look like a total dork. Like you were being mean for no reason. And pray for them. You might have to fake it a little at first, but our faith isn't about feeling, it's about obedience. God calls you to love your enemy, so you better figure out how. Psychologists say that you act your way into a new way of thinking instead of thinking your way into a new way of acting. Read that sentence again. As you keep on being nice, you might even forget what the war was all about in the first place. If nothing else, it will drive the other person nuts, trying to figure out why you are being so nice.

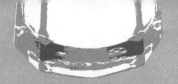

## >> Proverbs 27:1

There was this guy who was planning to break up with his wife, but he wanted to be a real jerk to her first. He and his buddies were really excited about it—they'd have all this time to hang after he got rid of the ol' ball and chain. So they talked about what would be the perfect plan for ruining her. They decided that he would just shower her with gifts and flowers and all kinds of sweet stuff before he broke it off. That way, she'd think things were going so great and then, wham!, out of nowhere he'd leave her. So that's what he did. For a full month he just laid it on thick.

So, when the time was about up, his friends checked on him to see how it was going. When they asked him when he'd be free, he looked at them like they were crazy. See, while he was doing all that awesome stuff for his lady, he fell in love with her all over again. The plan, you could say, was cancelled.

>> **Deuteronomy 5:29**

I wish their hearts would always respect me and that they would always obey my commands so that things would go well for them and their children forever! >>>>>>>>>>>>>>>>>>>>>>>>>

"Because I said so." Don't you hate those words? No reason why, no negotiating, just a plain and simple "because I said so." Sometimes we are expected to be obedient without an explanation. Of course there is a reason for it, one that we might not ever know until we stand before God and ask Him why. But by then we might not even care. In the meantime, we have to be content with obeying God's commands just "because He says so."

Right now you might not understand why there has to be a hell. You are going to have to go with the "because-I-said-so" answer from God until He chooses to reveal to you why it has to be. Sometimes your 'rents use those words because they need your obedience immediately and not your questions. You might have been in the middle of the street with a car coming at you. Your Mom yelled and expected you to move, not ask why. God wants our obedience without our always needing to know why. Can you live with that?

I beg you, brothers and sisters, by the name of our Lord Jesus Christ that all of you agree with each other and not be split into groups. I beg that you be completely joined together by having the same kind of thinking and the same purpose. ⟩ ⟩ ⟩ ⟩ ⟩

It totally bothered you the first time you showed up at church. Now it's not so much of a problem. That first time you walked into the room, everyone was in their own little groups. You didn't know anyone, and the friend who invited you hadn't shown up yet. Isolation! You finally saw someone you knew and tried to talk to them, but it was totally weird. You felt like you were invading a territory you knew nothing about, with people who really didn't care if you were there or not.

That was about three months ago. Since then everything has totally changed for you. You know a bunch of people, and you are always part of the group. You almost can't remember how it felt to be the outsider. What has happened is that you have integrated, but that doesn't mean the problem is gone. Every new person that comes in feels just what you felt. Different people, weird songs, and inside jokes are freaky stuff. Things changed for you because you stuck with it. Others might not give your group a chance because it's too hard.

At your next meeting spend at least five minutes talking with people you don't know. After talking with them for a while, take them with you as you talk to your friends. The more people they get to know, the better the unity within your ministry will be.

Then he said to Thomas, "Put your finger here, and look at my hands. Put your hand here in my side. Stop being an unbeliever and believe." Thomas said to him, "My Lord and my God!" Then Jesus told him, "You believe because you see me. Those who believe without seeing me will be truly happy." > > > > >

Is it really all true? Have you ever wondered about this thing we call Christianity? If you were to see Jesus today and he did a lot of cool miracles right in front of your eyes, then maybe, or at least probably, you would have no doubts about Him. But we don't get to see Jesus until we die, so for now there are times when you have to believe without seeing. There are times when it doesn't make much sense and you struggle to find the truth of what you believe, or even why you believe it.

It's okay to doubt. It might not feel good to doubt, but if one of Jesus' own followers wasn't completely convinced, it is okay to have times where you are less than sure. Those doubts are what help you exercise your faith. When you doubt, you have to search for answers. That is when faith plays such a major role. As your faith increases, your doubt decreases. Build on your faith, read about Jesus, talk to Him, and listen to what He says to you.

## >> Ephesians 4:3

You think ministry should be done a certain way, but your pastor has different ideas about it. Makes it kind of tough. You need each other. Without you and your friends, he has no one to help do ministry. Without him, you have no leader to guide and direct the ministry. What are the options? Anarchy is one. You could help lead a revolt against your pastor and do ministry your way and on your terms and only the way you want to do it. Or you could just quit being involved. Or you could talk to your pastor and find out the best way to work together. Listen to his vision and ideas for ministry. Then let him know the heart you have for your non-Christian friends and the ideas that you have to reach them for Jesus.

Don't cause trouble in your group. Don't publicly criticize your pastor. It won't do anything to help unify; it will more than likely divide. Listen, encourage, and lead. In his eyes, that's what will be the coolest part of ministering with you. How can you help and not be a problem?

>> **Galatians 5:6**

When we are in Christ Jesus, it is not important if we are circumcised or not. The important thing is faith—the kind of faith that works through love.

>>>>>>>>>>>>>>>>>>>>>>>>>>>>>

Punk. Prep. Drama queen. Cheerleader. Slacker. Every one of these words brings an image to your mind, right? I mean, you can picture exactly who I'm talking about. You've probably even got their personality pegged. It's pretty easy to judge someone based on their looks. It's even easier to just follow the stereotypes and avoid trying to get to know someone that's different from you.

Or are you the person who gets judged? Do you go to church and feel like you are always being watched? Well, here's the deal. Whatever group you fall into, what you look like, how you talk and how much Bible knowledge you have, it all has very little to do with your spirituality. How much you love God is not wrapped up in these external things. Sometimes we make the mistake of letting our church culture determine what sin is instead of the Bible. Paul tells us in this short verse that our faith is shown by our love of God and people. That is the most important aspect of our spirituality. So ask yourself this question: Do I love people or do I constantly judge them?

## >> Luke 1:28-30

The angel came to her and said, "Greetings! The Lord has blessed you and is with you." But Mary was very startled by what the angel said and wondered what this greeting might mean. The angel said to her, "Don't be afraid, Mary; God has shown you his grace." >>>>>>>>>>>>>>>>>>>>>>>>>>>

There is a lot of stuff out there about angels. Everything from television shows to greeting cards. It seems that the angel phenomenon is everywhere. Even people who don't really believe in God usually like the idea of angels. Angels are cool. They are real. They are the messengers of God. Do they appear to people today? Who really knows. How is that for a spiritual answer?

What I do know is this. Most times in the Bible where angels become visible, the person who sees the angel is scared stiff. It's not *Touched by an Angel* sentimentality. Most of the time the first words out of the angel's mouth are "Don't be afraid." That's a pretty big clue that there must be something totally intimidating about them! But there are instances in the Bible where angels appear and the person is completely oblivious.

So are some of the people you meet angels? You never know! Jesus told us to treat everyone as you would treat Him. It is a good rule to live by, since you never know just who you might be helping.

## >> Mark 14:50

You made the cut! You made it to the final casting of MTV's *The Real World*. As soon as everyone finds out, you become one of the most popular people at school. Local TV reporters interview you. A couple of your friends ask you to take them with you. Your newfound stardom rocks, so you think: Why not use it to your advantage? You're getting dates with the best-looking girls. Everyone wants to be your friend. People are saying how impressed they are with you and how you keep all of the fame in perspective. You aren't getting a big head at all.

The casting interviews are going strong, and you're on a roll. You've made it to the last twenty people. If they pick you, you will be on every TV in America and living in New York City. If you're not picked, you'll have to go back home with your parents. The names are called one by one. One by one your new friends from the casting group are called. But when they get to the end, you're standing in the loser section.

Suddenly everything has changed. No more cameras, no more interviews. You are not the most popular person anymore. In fact you've become a nobody. You feel alone and isolated. You now have an idea of how Jesus felt. Remember how you feel right now—it might come in handy when a friend ends up all alone sometime.

Defend the weak and the orphans; defend the rights of the poor and suffering. >>>>>>>>

I have always found it easier to pray for my friends when I know what is going on in their life. This means I gotta listen to them when they talk and probe a little, so I can really understand what's up. When you intercede to God for your buds, it can be general; but the specific stuff is cool 'cuz you can see those specific results in their lives.

Check this: *God, some days might not feel like it, but I know that every day of my life is a good day because of You. I am so grateful that You're my Dad. Don't give up on me, even though I mess up. I promise to trust You in everything I do.*

*I want to be obedient to You and that requires that I care about Your people. Help me to be a good listener, a safe person. I know I can be a little self-absorbed, but I want to turn away from that and be more like You. Teach me how to care for my friends and my enemies. I want to be a tool in Your hand, not scared, not stuck up, but weak and humble and ready to do whatever you ask.*

Also pray for us that God will give us an opportunity to tell people his message. Pray that we can preach the secret that God has made known about Christ. This is why I am in prison. ❯❯❯❯❯❯❯❯❯❯❯❯❯

Think about this: how many non-Christian friends do you have? If you answered zero, you need to pray for some, and look for them too. If you answered a lot, then you better start praying for more non-believers to come along and look for them, too. School is like the perfect place to find 'em. Don't be afraid to have non-Christian friends; you are called to be light in the darkness. Kind of hard to be light in the light. Don't hide God away and try to protect Him from the enemy. He has commanded you to get out there and share Him. Give Him away to those around you. You can't do that unless you talk with them. So make a plan to get to know some non-believers. Don't just plan to preach at them. Do what Jesus did. Love them. Help them. Pray for them. Then when the time is right, share Him with them. It won't be as hard as all that if you are truly loving them.

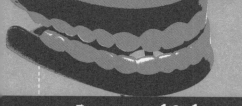

All of you must yield to the government rulers. No one rules unless God has given him the power to rule, and no one rules now without that power from God. >>>>>>>>>>>>>>>>>>>>>

Some of the hardest people to pray for are people who have power over you. Especially when you have just gotten a speeding ticket from them. But it's majorly important to pray for these people—cops, politicians, teachers—because they have a huge responsibility on their shoulders. Sometimes they are such jerks you have no desire to even think about them, let alone pray for them. But if you only pray for the people who are nice to you what good are you? Even evil people take care of their friends. So suck it up. God's command is clear. You gotta pray for people in authority, whether you like them or not. And you'll find out that when you pray for them, it's easier to submit to their authority, 'cuz you'll know that it's all in God's hands.

You are the light that gives light to the world. A city that is built on a hill cannot be hidden. >>>>>

## >> Matthew 5:14

How do you pray for the whole world? If you watch the news or read the paper, you know that this world is a long way from God. It's really a dark world out there. But have you ever noticed that when it is the darkest light seems to show up the most, to shine the brightest. I was once in a power outage and it was so dark that the light from my watch was like a flashlight.

Jesus made a lot of "I am" statements. "I am the truth . . . I am the way . . . . I am . . . you get it? The only "I am" statement that He also said we were is "the light of the world." You are the light of the world and that means you gotta shine.

But it ain't gonna be easy, I know. Remember to start with prayer, 'cuz with that anything is possible. No matter how dark the world gets, if we will only not be afraid and attempt to lighten up whatever darkness we can, then it will never get so dark as the enemy would like it to get. Think about what it means to bring light to darkness. Take a flashlight. Turn it on. Now turn out all the lights. What does the light do? Can there be darkness when there is light? Think about it.

75

## >> Numbers 20:12

But the LORD said to Moses and Aaron, "Because you did not believe me, and because you did not honor me as holy before the people, you will not lead them into the land I will give them." >>>>>>

What exactly does it mean to honor God? We are long past the days of animal sacrifice. The animals are safe, but what do *we* do? We honor God by showing every person we come into contact with that He is the number one priority in our life. Everything that we do, we keep God in mind. We honor our parents when we try to make them proud of us. We honor God when we try to make Him proud of how we live. Sometimes it is easy, and sometimes it is hard, but we should always try to have every part of our being speak of God.

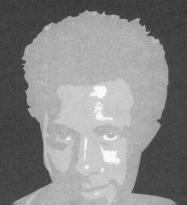

## >> 2 Timothy 1:5a

So what will the world say about you after you are gone? Ever thought about that? Let's take a look. Take a blank sheet of paper and write your own obituary. Write down all that you would want people to hear about you at the end of your life. Take a little time and think about it. After you have written it, don't read it. Turn the paper over and do this: Write your obituary again, only this time write down what is really going to be said about you. Don't lie. Write it from the perspective of someone else, like maybe someone who isn't that close to you. Maybe even ask someone to help you on this one. What would they say?

Now take the two and compare them. Are they both the same? You're living a pretty honest life. Are they different? Look carefully at how you're living your life. The second obituary is the one that is your true legacy.

## >> Micah 6:8

The LORD has told you, human, what is good; he has told you what he wants from you: to do what is right to other people, love being kind to others, and live humbly, obeying your God. >>>>>>>>>>

Don't you hate trying to figure out what other people expect of you? It's impossible to ever figure out. You can be minding your own business when *bam!* suddenly you've hacked someone off because you didn't do something that they thought you should do. Like getting doors. Who has that figured out? One girl expects you to get the door, while the other is totally ticked off when you do? And phone calls. One guy wants you to call him every day while another thinks that's just totally smothering. Face it, we'll never figure it out.

Good news. It doesn't work like that with God. He's told us exactly what He wants from us. He doesn't flip out and refuse to talk to us, and He doesn't try to punish us when we haven't done everything perfectly. Check out the great commandment (Mark 12:30-31) and the Great Commission (Matthew 28:18-20). He's pretty clear about what He's expecting isn't He? Spend time studying what God wants. His rules won't keep changing.

**I said to myself, "I will try having fun. I will enjoy myself." But I found that this is also useless.** >>>

## >> Ecclesiastes 2:1

It's Friday. You were a little late to school this morning and forgot your lunch on the way out the door. You've been kinda cranky 'cause you're so hungry. Last period is English, and when you find out you failed your biggest paper of the semester, you were really rude to the teacher. Looks like detention and summer school again. So you finally get home, you've been dreading having to tell your mom about your grades, and when you get there she's sitting in the kitchen crying. What's wrong? Your dog was run over today. You start to cry too, but you feel like a dork—it's just a dog. It's just that you've had such a crappy day.

So you call your buds to go party; you're gonna get your mind off it all. You say your "mantra" while you get ready—"tonight will be fun." But the party starts slow. There's really not much going on, the cutie from class doesn't show, and you're really just as depressed as you were this afternoon. You know, sometimes you just need to take time to deal. It's okay to stay at home and veg' with the family, or just spend some alone time in your room. Don't try to solve your probs by covering them up with "fun." Half the time the "fun" turns out to be pretty boring, and the problem always comes back to get you later. Deal with it head on—it's easier to just go ahead and get rid of it.

> Whoever loves money will never have enough money. Whoever loves wealth will not be satisfied with it . . . >>>>>>>>>>>>>>>>>>>>>>>>

## >> Ecclesiastes 5:10

You've seen it happen. Someone you've known since first grade suddenly stops coming to church stuff. You can't figure out why, so you ask them. Guess what? They say that they have too many bills, so they have to work. Got to pay for the car, cell phone, dates, insurance, pager, and ISP. They always seem to need more money. And they always have cash on them. You know because they like to flash it around, especially at youth group. It looks like they are trying to impress people with all their stuff. But you're not impressed. You just wish they would stay involved. Sometimes you wonder who is in control of their life, God or money. I mean, honestly, you have the rest of your life to work! And even then the cash shouldn't control your life.

How important is money to you? Do you feel like you have enough or are you always wanting more? Money can't buy you everything. Always wanting more is a sure way to be unhappy. Just read the verse again! Striving after money is useless. There are other more important ways you can be "rich." Can you think of some?

Because of this, since the day we heard about you, we have continued praying for you, asking God that you will know fully what he wants. We pray that you will also have great wisdom and understanding in spiritual things. >>>>>>>>>>>>>>>>>>>

It really throws everyone for a loop. You not only like watching your sister run cross-country, you actually cheer for her. You love to be encouraging and try to help her succeed. All your friends wonder how you do it. For them it would be too hard. After all, you hold all the school records in cross-country—what if she takes them away? You don't care about that. In fact, you love your sister and you want her to do as well or better than you did! You'd love it if she broke—no, shattered!—all the records you set.

It is hard for some of us to imagine any person wanting to see a rival succeed. Most of the time we see star athletes who want their records to be preserved for all time. They don't want anyone to even approach the marks they've achieved. Pray and ask God to bless your friends in new and exciting ways. Don't be satisfied with just a selfish prayer—a "bless them as you bless me" prayer. Pray for God to give greater blessings to people around you.

Knowledge puffs you up with pride, but love builds up. >>>>>>>>>>>>>>>>>>>>>>>>>>>>

You have been watching your pastor for a few months and think it's time to let him know just where he is wrong in his theology. You have done your research—listened to tapes, read commentaries, studied the history. You know that his interpretation of a verse in Revelation is completely wacked. You are going to tell him exactly why you are right and he is wrong.

You go in unannounced and tell him the way you see the passage. You tell him how you have been taught to interpret the Bible, and how he is way off base. You fall just short of demanding a retraction from him the next time he speaks.

You're surprised to find him listening so intently to you. He wants to know how things are going in your life. "How is the roller hockey?" he asks as he listens to you. You want to stay on the subject. Your pastor shows you what the original language says and how it is a common mistake to interpret it the way you did. His appreciation of you listening and paying attention makes you feel great about him, and lousy about how you handled the situation.

Which one describes you more—knowledge or love?

But Peter said to Jesus, "Lord, I am ready to go with you to prison and even to die with you!" But Jesus said, "Peter, before the rooster crows this day, you will say three times that you don't know me." >>

What would you do to get into a sold-out concert of your fave band? True story: these two guys from Bosnia wanted to see U2 really, really bad. In fact, they were trying to interview Bono for TV in Sarajevo. Well, their country was at war, so what did they have to do to get to the concert? Cross a war zone, ride in a boat across the Adriatic Sea, and persuade some pretty tough security guards to let them in the manager's dressing room with their cameras. No small feat. But they did it—and got to hang out with the band at a post-concert party.

What would you do to go to church? What would you do to talk to Jesus? Would you do what these guys from Bosnia did? Would you even think about it? Think hard about what you'd be willing to do for Christ. And think hard about what He was willing to do for you.

He took his stick in his hand and chose five smooth stones from a stream. He put them in his shepherd's bag and grabbed his sling. Then he went to meet the Philistine. >>>>>>>>>>>>>>>>>>>

What do you do when you are facing a major obstacle? How do you react? Do you hide? Do you avoid? What do you do?

It might be a big test. Maybe it is a competition that you are preparing for. A big game, an audition, an interview, or even a hot date. Whatever the case, we all handle tough situations in totally different ways.

The whole Israeli army was scared of Goliath and his tormenting. He challenged the army to a fight every day, and no one accepted. That is, until David showed up. David figured that with five small stones and one big God, the giant would be dust before the day was over. David didn't just think it, he fully believed it, acted on it, and saw it happen. And in the end, he didn't need the five stones, he only needed one. So why not try that approach? Go find one smooth stone and put it where you will always see it. Look at it—especially when you have something big coming up. Remember to tell yourself that with God everything will turn out all right.

It really isn't a big deal. Their insurance will pay for it anyway. So you decide to steal a few car stereos, thinking that it won't hurt anyone. Besides, it is an easy way to make some quick cash, and you really need some if you want to go to that concert next month. You and your friends set up an elaborate plan. Each one of you plays a different part in making sure that you are able to get the stereos quickly and without a hitch. After you do a couple of jobs a funny thing happens. You find it kind of fun. The rush of getting away with it is an adrenaline high like you have never experienced before. This makes it all the more cool, doing something that makes you feel like you're in a different world.

It's a lot of fun until you get caught. Now it's your worst nightmare, getting handcuffed and sent to jail. Yeah it was fun, but the fun you experienced wasn't nearly as high as the low you're having now. You have to tell your parents, you have a record, and you might get expelled from school. Sin's fun—the devil has to do something to make it tempting to us. But what are the consequences of your sin?

Amaziah did what the Lord said was right, but he did not really want to obey him. >>>>>>>>

Potential. It really doesn't mean a whole lot unless you do something with it. It's like having a great set of car keys and no car. Having the best snowboard money can buy and living in the Sahara desert. Maybe you have one of the highest IQ's in your school, but your grades wouldn't agree.

The word "potential" might describe what kind of ministry you are having in the lives of your friends. You are with them every day but never feel the need to tell them about who Jesus is. God is working on your heart and renewing your mind, but it all stays inside you. You choose not to share it with any of them.

Amaziah does it even though he doesn't want to. He obeys because that's what he's supposed to do. But sometimes, when we obey, even when our souls feel dry, we'll be given a passion stronger than we've ever had before. Work on figuring out what the key is that will get you excited about God again, then unlock your potential for Him.

Now may God himself, the God of peace, make you pure, belonging only to him. May your whole self—spirit, soul, and body—be kept safe and without fault when our Lord Jesus Christ comes.

>> i Thessalonians 5:23

>>>>>>>>>>>>>>>>>>>>>>>>>>>

Tattoo or no tattoo, that is the question. Isn't it? Tattoos and body piercing are hot, but the 'rents aren't real crazy about them. "Your body is a temple of God," they say. "True the body is a temple, but I'm not above decorating my place of worship," you reply.

The "body is a temple" means you don't do things that mess with what God has created. It's easy to say that it is better to get earrings than to eat like a pig all the time. The piercing doesn't destroy like gluttony. But what about all that metal that's leaking into your system from the rod in your tongue? Think about that. It can't be good for you.

Could you be destroying your body and not even realize it?

No matter the final answer, here's the deal—you live with your parents. They are responsible for you. So what they say goes. Your first responsibility is to honor God, who says "Honor your parents." So check yourself. Your 'rents might be totally off on this one, but as long as they are responsible for you, you gotta give them some respect. When you are on your own, you can consider your body and how you should treat it, but for now submit and allow your parents to have the last word; it will honor God and them.

You know that in a race all the runners run, but only one gets the prize. So run to win! All those who compete in the games use self-control so they can win a crown. That crown is an earthly thing that lasts only a short time, but our crown will never be destroyed.

>>>>>>>>>>>>>>>>>>>>>>>>>

Sarah hates to lose. When she competes she becomes another person. It doesn't matter what the game or competition, she just refuses to give in. She is next to impossible to be near when she is in "competitive mode." Cards, car racing, cross-country running, or miniature golf—she has to win.

Sarah is so competitive that most of her friends stop hanging around her and quit asking her to do stuff. She is out of control. But Sarah starts realizing that her competitiveness is getting the best of her. She notices that she isn't getting invited out anymore, and when she competes, everyone roots against her. Sarah realizes that God is not getting glorified by the way she competes. She makes a decision and changes the focus in her life.

Now, instead of hating to lose games, she focuses on hating seeing her friends not know God. She even put her favorite Bible verse on her favorite trophy to remind her that people matter, not sports. How competitive are you for God?

You will know these people by what they do. Grapes don't come from thornbushes, and figs don't come from thorny weeds. In the same way, every good tree produces good fruit, but a bad tree produces bad fruit. > > > > > > > > > > > > > > > > > > > > > > >

Orange, apple, papaya. What kind of fruit are you? It sounds like a bad question, but in light of what Jesus gets at in His message in Matthew, it's legit. Okay, it might not be fair to ask if you are a fruit or not, but rather what kind of fruit are you producing?

The kind of fruit that a Christian produces is love, joy, peace, patience, kindness, goodness, faithfulness, gentleness, and self-control (Galatians 5:22-23). Do you see any of these qualities coming out of your life? If you see none of these in your life, you are not being productive. If you are trying to prevent these qualities from being evident in your life, you are being counter-productive. Your life as a believer in Jesus should produce fruit as evidence that you love God and the people around you. If you're not seeing any fruit, you probably need to address the situation. Find a ministry to plug in to, so that you can cultivate your own life in a way that will produce fruit. Buy some toy fruit at a store and put it in your room as a symbol to remind you that your life should be producing fruit, and lots of it.

> We do not enjoy being disciplined. It is painful, but later, after we have learned from it, we have peace, because we start living in the right way.

## >> Hebrews 12:11

>>>>>>>>>

Seth loved to push the limits of what his parents would allow. One night he was out with some friends and they went to a party. Seth knew it was wrong, but what were his parents going to do? What they didn't know wouldn't hurt them. And besides, he had no intention of getting caught.

At about 11:30, Seth needed to go pick up his girlfriend, who was sneaking out of her house to come to the party. He rode with some friends, and they parked the car where she was supposed to meet them. The guys ran into the woods to pee, and Seth waited. She was running a little late, but that was typical. He watched a car pull up and thought it was some more guys. When he looked up he realized he was wrong. Before he knew it he was breathing a 1.1 into the cop's breathalyzer. Even though he wasn't driving, he got busted.

He was taken down to the station and booked, then he was allowed to call his parents. They were not happy. He lost his license to drive and insurance for one year. He also had to take several driver's ed classes and go to counseling for a year. During that year he learned his lesson.

Doing the right thing is a lot easier than trying not to get caught. Live your life right.

In the same way, you husbands should live with your wives in an understanding way, since they are weaker than you. But show them respect, because God gives them the same blessing he gives you—the grace that gives true life. Do this so that nothing will stop your prayers. > > > > > > > > > > > > > > > >

Kind of a strange verse for a student to read. There probably aren't a lot of you that have to deal with your husband or wife. We could discuss the implications of the "weaker" person in this verse, but that isn't what this is about. Let's look at the last sentence. What do you find as distractions to your prayers? Let's take it one step further. What things are distractions to your spiritual life? How about the distractions in your friends' spiritual lives?

One thing that you will notice as you go through life is this: If you're not careful, gaining a boy/girlfriend can be a serious distraction to your relationship with God. It is hard to not let it be. It feels a lot better to spend an extra two hours a day with someone who loves being with you over reading your Bible and praying. Don't let the distraction set in. Keep your boy/girlfriend, but don't neglect your most important relationship. God will be there forever, that girlfriend may only last another week. Choose wisely.

But the people were very thirsty for water, so they grumbled against Moses. They said, "Why did you bring us out of Egypt? Was it to kill us, our children, and our farm animals with thirst?" >>

Cassie was the kind of girl that everyone was captivated by. She could get everything done—she was a great leader. But, she was a constant, low-level grumbler. She would grumble about anything, no matter how insignificant it was. When she went on a date with Rick, they had a great time together. When people asked her about it the next day, she would tell them "It was fun, but Rick was late picking me up." True, Rick was five minutes late, but that is nothing compared to having a great time together.

Even her ministry wasn't immune from her grumbling. One night during an event that Cassie had planned, six high school students gave their life to Jesus. It was a night of great emotion as most of these students had been prayed for by their friends for a long time. Instead of being excited about the kingdom building that took place, Cassie was upset that the balloons were the wrong color and that her youth pastor used a different verse in his message than the one she gave him.

Chronic grumbling prevents you from seeing all the good God is doing around you. Don't believe me? Just read the book of Exodus. Focus on what is right; there are enough people in this world that will tell you what is wrong.

As the crowd grew larger, Jesus said, "The people who live today are evil. They want to see a miracle for a sign, but no sign will be given them, except the sign of Jonah."

>>>>>>>>>>>>>>>

Have you ever watched *A Baby Story* on TLC? It is pretty interesting. You get to see the whole ordeal many people go through just to have a baby. Some people will tell you that they would believe in God if they could just see a miracle performed in front of them. The truth is, miracles are happening all around us!

The problem is ours. We have witnessed so many "amazing things" in our lifetime, that we have become callous to miracles. If you need to see a miracle, watch *A Baby Story*. A miracle happens on every episode when another life is brought into the world. Don't get fooled into believing that it's not a miracle—just watch the parents' reaction!

Here's another miracle you can see: Watch someone come to faith in Jesus. It is truly a miracle—watching a person walk from death to eternal life. It might require you to talk to them about Jesus, but trust me, the conversation will be worth the miracle you see.

Then God said to Moses, "I AM WHO I AM. When you go to the people of Israel, tell them, 'I AM sent me to you.'" >>>>>>>>>>>>>>>>>>>>>>>>>>

J. Lo. Madonna. Bono. Mandy. Britney. Justin. Sting.

Some names mean absolutely nothing, they are simply cool to have. Some people like their name, others try to go by a nickname, and others try to change their name altogether. Watch names and see how they change through generations. Names that were popular a hundred years ago are now becoming popular again.

What do you think of when you think of God's name? When you see Him face to face you're probably not going to go, "Hey God, how ya doin'?" Then again, you probably won't say "Hey, I AM, how ya doin'?" either. God's name is significant because it directly represents who He is. He is "I AM."

Explanation: He is everything you need Him to be. God may not be everything you want Him to be, but He will always be everything you need. His name is directly related to His qualities.

Think of everything you want God to be. Now think of everything you need God to be in your life. His name is directly related to what you need Him to be. He is the great "I AM."

Then Gideon said to God, "Don't be angry with me if I ask just one more thing. Please let me make one more test. Let only the wool be dry while the ground around it gets wet with dew." That night God did that very thing. Just the wool was dry, but the ground around it was wet with dew. >>>>>

Maybe you aren't praying specifically enough. How often have you said the prayer "God bless this food." Think about it—how exactly do you want God to bless your food? How about this: You have a test and you give God the "help-me-do-well-on-this-test" prayer. You get the test back with a C+ on it. You're upset that you didn't do better, but God did answer your prayer. It's kind of like asking your parents for money. If you say "Dad, can I have some money?" and he gives you a nickel. He did answer your request. You have no right to be offended by the amount. Back to the prayer for the test. If you wanted an A, you should have prayed for an A.

Remember, just because you pray for it to happen doesn't guarantee it will happen. God might answer you with a no. Realize that His answer might have been no for that specific prayer, but He doesn't always answer no. Pray specifically and look for specific answers.

God once said, "Let the light shine out of the darkness!" This is the same God who made his light shine in our hearts by letting us know the glory of God that is in the face of Christ. >>>>>>>>>>>

You couldn't help noticing the difference in Carmen. Two years ago she was negative and extremely moody. She felt like nothing ever went right in her life, and the frowns on her face made people want to stay away from her. It seemed like she was always talking about her parents' divorce. She was a Christian, but there didn't seem to be happiness in her heart.

One year at a retreat, she broke. God got a hold of her life, and she could really feel His presence around her. It wasn't anything that she could explain very well, but it was obvious to those people around her that something was different. Yes, she still had to daily deal with life's frustrations. But God was making a difference in her life. Now people called her and wanted to be around her. She made an effort to spend time with God at least four times a week, and she talked to Him constantly.

People wanted to know what happened! How could they make God that real in their own lives? Carmen's life was changing for the better because she realized who God really was to her. What do people notice about you? Does it draw them closer to God or push them away from Him?

But Ruth said, "Don't beg me to leave you or to stop following you. Where you go, I will go. Where you live, I will live. Your people will be my people, and your God will be my God. > > > > > > > > * > > > >

Alex was a little confused. When asked what and where she considered "home," she didn't quite know how to answer. You see, she came from a broken family. She had lived with her mom and stepfather, then decided she would move in with her real dad. Things weren't working out and her dad asked her to leave. Not wanting to go back with Mom, she moved in with Grandma and Grandpa. They had so many rules that Alex never felt totally comfortable. She ended up spending the majority of her time at her older sister's apartment. Now you figure it out—where would Alex call home?

Thirty years ago, home was a little easier to define. Today it isn't so simple. There are so many places we could call home, but don't feel like home. There are other places that we feel at home, yet it isn't really the place we would label our home.

Where is home for you? Your friends? Your church? God? What would you say defines or makes up a home? It doesn't mean a house or apartment anymore, so what is it for you today?

> You guide the people. but you are blind! You are like a person who picks a fly out of a drink and then swallows a camel! >>>>>>>>>>>>>

Here is your mission: Go the next twenty-four hours without judging anyone. Have one day where you accept anyone for anything, withholding love and care from no one. See if you can do it. Make it a goal. After you have done it once, what is keeping you from doing it again? Deal with your own issues instead of holding everyone else's issues against them.

## >> Matthew 18:21-22

Then Peter came to Jesus and asked, "Lord, when my fellow believer sins against me, how many times must I forgive him? Should I forgive him as many as seven times?" Jesus answered, "I tell you, you must forgive him more than seven times. You must forgive him even if he wrongs you seventy times seven." > > > > > > > > > > > > > > > > > > > > > > > > > >

How much more can you take? Every time you go out with Jenny, all she does is put you down! You can handle it to a point, but sometimes she gets carried away, and expects to see you laugh it off. She gives you the "you need to lighten up," or "I'm just joking" lines so often that you hardly believe her. When the two of you aren't around other people she is one of the nicest people in the whole world.

You've brought the issue up with her, and she always apologizes. She lets you know that it's just the way she relates to people. You forgive her, but are getting tired of how she treats you around other people. You think about just finding someone new to hang out with. You then realize that you really like Jenny, and you know that you can help her change with your patience and forgiveness.

Don't give up on hard friends. Lead and show them how life can really be lived. Loving people is the key.

It is easy to sit off to the side and be amused by their actions. You know the type of people: those who say they are leaders but nobody will follow them. (It's really hard to lead no one.) They say all of the right things and make you believe they know what they're doing, but honestly they couldn't lead a balloon if they were pulling it on a string. Actually, it's sad. They might be good at it if they would only apply themselves. But they don't. The only thing they work at is getting out of doing any work!

Not only don't they lead, but they can't follow. When a job needs to get done, they are very quick to tell other people how it's done, but they are not willing to do it. When you look for them, they are nowhere to be found. When you finally spot them, they are eating doughnuts and drinking pop. Meanwhile, you organized everything and got the job done. Listen, if you have the gift of leadership, use it by getting involved. If you don't, that's cool too. Become a loyal follower, and do what is asked of you.

Do not look out only for yourselves. Look out for the good of others also. > > > > > > > > > > > > >

Okay, let's be honest here. You want to date someone who is hot. Like it or not, physical attraction is what gets the whole dating thing going. The nice thing about physical attraction is that it means different things to different people. Some like blue eyes while others like brown. One person likes long hair over short. You might not feel like you measure up to the models in magazines, but chances are you measure up for someone, and that is good. Everyone has different taste. But after looks or attraction, what is there?

You might say personality or character, and those are both good. But think about this: What do others see in you that would make them want to go out with you? We can spend all our time looking for the right person in our life, but if we are not working at being the right person, we're wasting our time. We will probably not be able to keep a boy/girlfriend. You might land a date with the best-looking hottie in the whole school (to you, that is), but if you're a jerk, forget it, they'll never go out with you again.

Life isn't fulfilled by finding the right person, but by being the right person.

## >> Matthew 5:37

Rachel will tell anyone anything they want to hear. If her friend has a problem, Rachel will tell them she'll call that night. But she won't. It happens a lot. You start to get sick of it. Every time you give her a chance, she goes and blows it. She is very likable, but she will tell you anything you want to hear, whether she means it or not.

One day she says that she is quitting her job because she is tired of how her boss treats her. You cut class and talk with her for the rest of the day. The next day you hear that she is asking for some extra hours at work because she enjoys the place so much! What's the deal? You wish once, just once, you could feel like you are getting the straight story from her. You feel like she is constantly letting you down with her "hollow" words.

What about you? Have you ever let people down by what you said? How can you prevent it? Buy a container of "super glue" and put the words "my words" in black ink on the outside of the tube. Let it always remind you to make your words stick. Say what you mean and mean what you say.

>> **Ephesians 4:31-32**

Do not be bitter or angry or mad. Never shout angrily or say things to hurt others. Never do anything evil. Be kind and loving to each other, and forgive each other just as God forgave you in Christ. >>>

They may be the weirdest or most annoying people you know, but you are stuck with them. They are your siblings, and they are yours for life. Right now they may just be your punching bags or you may be theirs. If you have to fight with them use these rules:

- Don't run to your parents about every little squabble. Your brother might, but you try to keep it to just the siblings.
- Concentrate on solving the problem, not passing the blame. Fight the issue, not the person.
- It's not a name-calling contest. Sticks and stones, blah blah blah.
- No physical contact. Hitting your brother just makes him want to hit you back. If you get hit, walk away until you both have cooled down enough to concentrate on rule #2.
- Learn to say "I'm sorry." It is hard for the fight to continue when you own up to being wrong. If you are wrong (honestly) then admit it.
- No scorekeeping. If you keep records of who does what constantly then you never really forgive, instead you hold a grudge.
- Find a different outlet for your anger than your siblings. It's not their fault your girlfriend broke up with you.
- No stupid fights. Who cares who was sitting in the chair first—there is more furniture in the house.

Follow these rules for fighting with your siblings and you just might see your relationship with them improve.

So, my son, do what I say. My brother Laban is living in Haran. Go to him at once! Stay with him for a while, until your brother is not so angry. >>>>

"It would be easier if I were away from here," Steve muttered quietly to himself. The thought of running away from home and starting life over somewhere else felt so appealing. Steve had burned a lot of bridges recently. His girlfriend broke up with him, and instead of getting on with his life, Steve decided to trash her. When she started dating a new guy, he also became a victim of Steve's wrath. Now the new guy and Steve were getting ready to fight over it, and Steve knew he was in trouble. To make matters worse, Steve missed his curfew and his dad took away the car for a month. It really felt like it couldn't get much worse for him. In all honesty, Steve wished he could do things over, but the damage was too severe now. There just didn't seem to be any way out. The only option he could come up with was to hit the road.

Steve is like a lot of people. At times all of us feel that things would be so much better if we could just get away. Here's the problem with that: you might be in a new place, but you will stay the same person. Just because your location changes doesn't mean you change. You have to start by changing some of your habits.

Steve realized this and went back to apologize to his ex-girlfriend. That started the ball rolling on changing some habits in his life. What do you need to change?

Christ himself suffered for sins once. He was not guilty, but he suffered for those who are guilty to bring you to God. His body was killed, but he was made alive in the spirit. > > > > > > > > > > > > > >

It's almost funny how we try to rank sin. Here's the idea: Stealing a cookie is far lower on the "sin scale" than stealing a car. Pre-marital sex is not as bad as having an affair on your spouse. But an affair is better than having a homosexual relationship. Why do we do this? Perhaps it's because we try to think of sin like we think of breaking the law. In our world we have a justice system that ranks offenses and punishes according to the severity of the crime. If you speed, you pay a fine. If you drive drunk, that's worse. Now you pay a fine, lose your license, and maybe go to jail.

So we use this line of thinking when we look at sin—doing things that God doesn't like. It makes us feel better to compare ourselves to others. We don't feel so guilty about messing up in God's eyes if we think the guy sitting next to us in church has done something worse. But we are just fooling ourselves!

All sin is equal. So was the attack on the World Trade Center worse than the lie you told your sister this morning? There was definitely a bigger effect from the World Trade Center—thousands of lives were lost. But Jesus died for both of them, equally. If there had been no attack, He would have still died for your lie. Quit trying to rate or justify what you do wrong and own up to it with God. Let Him know you messed up and that you want His forgiveness.

## >> Hebrews 12:14-15

Try to live in peace with all people, and try to live free from sin. Anyone whose life is not holy will never see the Lord. Be careful that no one fails to receive God's grace and begins to cause trouble among you. A person like that can ruin many of you. >>>>>>>>>>>>>>>>>>>>>>>>>

Have you wondered if your family is ever going to get better? Maybe you feel stuck—this is the best your family will ever be so you'd better just make the best of it. Mom is nosy, Dad is distant, and your sister, well, she is just plain annoying. There are times when you find yourself praying, "God, why did you put me with these people?" You know what? You are not the first person to ever pray that, and you won't be the last either. Face it, though, these people will be with you for the rest of your life, and you can't get around it. Simply coping with them will not make it better, although it might maintain your sanity.

If you really want to make your family better, it might fall on you to do it. You will have to be the one that makes attempts to extend grace to these people when you feel like they need to extend it to you. Your focus should be on what you can give to make your family better, not what you can get.

Brandon and his friends were hanging out downtown one night, just kicking it. As Brandon was talking with his friends, leaning up against a light post, he heard the screech of tires coming to a quick stop. When he looked up he saw Kristi sitting in a still car in the middle of moving traffic. Brandon and Kristi had been friends for a while, but he never dreamed he would be able to go out with her. She was popular and he was, well, he was just Brandon. Kristi looked at Brandon and yelled "get in." And so he did! She drove up to the overlook of the city. She asked him if they could kiss and he instantly agreed. They kissed a couple of times, but it was getting late so they had to go. Brandon called Kristi the next day and they ended up spending the whole weekend together. They were now officially a couple and Brandon couldn't believe it, because this was Kristi.

By Monday, Brandon and Kristi told each other that they were in love. They really believed it at the time. But within one month, they couldn't stand each other. Too much too fast, and it destroyed their relationship. Now they aren't even friends.

What happened? They got carried away with their feelings. Be wise and think—be careful, because your feelings can sometimes lie to you.

107

>> **1 Corinthians 13:4-5**

Love is patient and kind. Love is not jealous, it does not brag, and it is not proud. Love is not rude, is not selfish, and does not get upset with others. Love does not count up wrongs that have been done. >>>>>>>>>>>>

You have just read how to make relationships work through love. Let's re-write this passage and see how you can ruin any relationship for sure:

*Be pushy and mean. Get jealous of all that you see others do and say. Brag about how great you are, and never listen to others when they have something significant to say. Be proud that you know more than anyone else and brag about it as well. Be rude as often as you can, putting down and embarrassing those you want to be around. Everything in this world is yours, so take it, being as selfish as you want, getting mad every time others try to take a place higher than you. Above all else, keep score. When someone messes up with you and asks forgiveness, tell them they are forgiven and then use the event to manipulate your position over them in the future.*

Do this and every relationship in your life will go sour.

108

Friends. You love 'em and, at times, you hate them. But your close ones, the ones you hang out with the most, you believe you will always love. Think about your group of friends. Is one of these types in your circle?

*The Sucker*: These friends drain you emotionally. Everything in their life is tragic and they wear you out. The plus side? These friends are always caring and compassionate.

*The Gabber*: They talk all the time. Sometimes they don't even know what they are talking about, but they still talk. Talk, talk, talk, talk, talk. The plus side is that you feel like your ear matters to them.

*The Schemer*: Practical joker and life of the party. This is the creative person you hang out with. They can be a little moody, but they are generally the liveliest person in your circle.

*The Slammer*: They put everyone and everything down. The one good part of this is that they can usually talk their way through anything, even when it appears you're going to get in trouble.

*The Protector*: This person would die for you. They will make sure everyone in your group is always protected. You always feel safe around them.

Love each other like brothers and sisters. Give each other more honor than you want for yourselves.

>>>>>>>>>>>>>>>>>>>>>>>>>>>>>>>>

## >> Romans 12:10

A question almost everyone asks as they go through life is "How can I make a relationship last?" It's an honest question that deserves some attention. Paul, when he wrote to the Romans, expressed a key quality in helping to make a relationship last: "Give each other more honor than you want for yourselves." There it is.

Here's some ways you can honor others: Try not getting jealous when you see them talking with someone else. Insecurity on your part can be a big turn off to someone who may like you. Jealousy, when left alone, will eventually turn into possessiveness. If you get to the point where you have to know the whereabouts of the other person every moment, this will drive you crazy. Lighten up and allow people to be independent and develop friendships away from you. Lastly, honor people by not getting lazy in your relationship with them. Relationships take work and if only one person is working, then it isn't much of a relationship at all.

Honoring other people isn't always easy, but it always pays off.

Not all those who say that I am their Lord will enter the kingdom of heaven. The only people who will enter the kingdom of heaven are those who do what my Father in heaven wants. >>>>>>>>

Playing head games with God is not advisable. You know what head games are—when you tell people everything they want to hear and never intend to follow through with any of it. Most of the time we see head games happen in relationships between guys and girls. Girls will lead a guy on, making him think she's interested. Then when he asks her out, she introduces him to her boyfriend. But guys are not above playing the game either. Guys can make girls think they will call or take them out only to get the girl off his back. He will only call if every other option goes bad.

Head games are a part of life. We have had them played on us, and we probably have played them on someone else. They're deceitful and show a lack of integrity.

We also play these games with God. We tell a lot of people that He is our God, but in reality, we only use Him when it is convenient. We don't do what God wants, we do what we want and then claim it is God's will, knowing fully that God had no part in the action. Quit playing games with God. Don't just say He is a priority, make Him the priority.

You should teach people whom you can trust the things you and many others have heard me say. Then they will be able to teach others. ⟩⟩⟩⟩⟩

## ⟩⟩ 2 Timothy 2:2

Their relationship developed a lot over the four years that they were together. Shelley was a woman in her mid-twenties, married and volunteering her time in the high school ministry at her church. Naomi was in the eighth grade when she first moved into the high school ministry. One of Naomi's first events with the group was something called the "frozen food challenge," and it was here that she met Shelley for the first time. In the course of the evening Shelley could see something in Naomi—she wanted to deepen her relationship with God.

Shelley asked Naomi if she would join her small group. Naomi agreed and then began a journey that would last four years, but the lessons would last a lifetime. As the small group met weekly, Naomi got more and more involved, growing in her relationship with God. During her senior year it wasn't uncommon for Shelley to have Naomi facilitate the entire group time, and Naomi loved it.

Now Naomi has graduated and wonders what will happen next year when she goes off to college. Hopefully Naomi will look at Shelley's life and determine to do the same thing. There is one thing clear about the scenario: We all need to be fed spiritually. At the same time, we also need to be feeding others. Don't try to pour yourself into others without being poured into and don't have someone pour into your life without you giving back as well.

## >> Deuteronomy 10:19

You might be to the point in your life where you are wondering if you really need your family anymore. You might think it'd be easier to not have them around. Being on your own would be so much simpler than having to worry about constantly telling Mom and Dad exactly where you are going, and when, and with whom, and why. It'd be better than getting mad because your sister borrowed your clothes and ruined them. Living by yourself would give you freedom to watch whatever you want on TV! All in all, wouldn't it be better to be away from these people?

Actually, maybe not. Moving away from your family would bring up a new set of frustrations and responsibilities: money, bills, roommates, just to start. You see, being on your own may not be the answer to your family frustrations, it just looks good from a distance.

Learn to live well with your family. It will teach you the skills you need to get along with people outside of your family. People like co-workers, roommates, and friends. The skills you learn in your family relationships will last a lifetime. Take advantage of those skills.

113

Those who work their land will have plenty of food, but the one who chases empty dreams is not wise.
>>>>>>>>>>>>>>>>>>>>>>>>>>>>>

## >> Proverbs 12:11

Jerome loves football. He has played his whole life. When he was around five years old, his brother used to take him to play with the older kids in the neighborhood, mainly because Jerome was so good. As he got older, his skills really started to develop. He was an incredible passer, spending every night out in his backyard throwing footballs late into the evening, until his mom would call him in for bed. Jerome would watch games on TV and listen to the post-game interviews. He was always encouraged, hearing the phrase "If you put your mind to it, you can accomplish anything." So Jerome tried harder to be better at football because he wanted to play in the NFL. There was one slight problem: Jerome was only five feet tall as a junior in high school. He got cut from the team. Instead of falling apart, Jerome found other skills to develop and moved on with his life.

"If you put your mind to it, you can accomplish anything" that's within God's will for your life. We all have dreams that don't work out. Take what you learn and apply it to accomplishing different and greater goals. Don't fall apart! Always apply what you learn and look for God to lead.

David asked, "Is anyone still left in Saul's family? I want to show kindness to that person for Jonathan's sake!" >>>>>>>>>>>>>>>>>>>>>>>>>>

You and Jennie are together all the time. She's your best friend. You have a ton of inside jokes, you can cry on her shoulder (or vice versa) whenever there's a problem, she gives you little notes in class with Bible verses on them for encouragement. She's the perfect best friend, and you know that y'all will be best friends forever.

Except for her family. To put it nicely, they're jerks. They're really rude to you. They say the meanest things about all your other friends. They totally control Jennie—no calls after 7:30, one TV show a week, no rated-R movies, and on and on. And the worst thing is, her stepfather's your science teacher. So he knows all the kids, he picks on you in class, and you totally think he grades your tests unfairly.

David and Jonathan were best friends, but Jonathan's dad (Saul) was trying to kill David. Did David get all ticked at Jonathan and quit being friends with him because he couldn't take his terrible dad? No way. When he found out that Jonathan's dad died, David mourned for him.

Find out how you can be nice to Jennie's family. When you spend the night, read her little brother a story before he goes to bed. Help her plan her mom's surprise birthday. Do what it takes to show them God's love.

"Then the King will answer, 'I tell you the truth, anything you did for even the least of my people here, you also did for me.'" >>>>>>>>>>>>

Do you realize that there are a lot of people out there that we need to show kindness to? There are people all over your town, county, state, nation, and world that need help. So why don't we do something about it? It might be because we don't want to know about it—it makes us scared to think about their problems. We have adopted the "don't ask, don't tell" philosophy into our everyday lives. If we don't currently know what needs are out there, then we don't want to find out because we already have enough concerns to invest in. We don't look for new ways in which we can help those who desperately need it.

How have you done that in your life? Do you go out looking for people to help or do you try to avoid them? Think of how many more people we could reach out to if we went looking to extend our hand to them. Don't wait for them to come to you, go to them. Who needs your touch and care today? What are you going to do about it?

## >> Luke 21:1-4

As Jesus looked up, he saw some rich people putting their gifts into the Temple money box. Then he saw a poor widow putting two small copper coins into the box. He said, "I tell you the truth, this poor widow gave more than all those rich people. They gave only what they did not need. This woman is very poor, but she gave all she had to live on."

>>>>>>>>>>>>>>>>>>>>>>>>>>>>>

Take two pennies and tape them together. Put them in your wallet, purse, or whatever you use to hold your money. Every time you see these two pennies, ask yourself this question: If this is all I had to live on, would I give it to God? It is easy to give to God out of our abundance, but do we give to God out of our poverty?

As a student, you probably don't think that you have much to give God. So you might not give at all. What God really wants you to give is your life. After that, He wants to know that He has your heart. That is why we give, even when it is hard. That shows God that He has our heart. When we don't feel like we can give, but do it anyway, we show God how important He is to us.

Look at your pennies and ask the question again. How important is God to you?

Each one should give as you have decided in your heart to give. You should not be sad when you give, and you should not give because you feel forced to give. God loves the person who gives happily. >>

You couldn't figure it out. Every time Brittany put money in the offering at church, she would laugh out loud—at least loud enough for the people around her to hear it. She also did it whenever she got asked to help out with various activities around the church. She would simply start laughing and then, usually, say yes.

One day, you finally asked her, "Why do you always laugh?" She answered that she doesn't always laugh, she only laughs when she gives something to God. It helps her remember that God loves a gift from a cheerful heart. The reasoning might sound stupid to other people, but Brittany found it to be helpful. It reminded her that what she was giving was really not hers anyway! God gave her everything she had, so she always gave back when she had the chance. The laughing just puts it into the right perspective for her.

Try it sometime. Watch the reaction of the people around you as you laugh, putting money in the church collection. The people around you might think you're strange, but God won't!

Which one of these two men best represents you and your life? On the outside, does everything look great? Do you consider yourself to be one of the godliest people around, while on the inside you know that your life is as fake as it can get? Or are you unmasked enough that you can own up to your faults and ask God to forgive you? In other words, does who you see on the inside of your life match who you are on the outside? Why or why not?

Jesus told this story to some people who thought they were very good and looked down on everyone else: "A Pharisee and a tax collector both went to the Temple to pray. The Pharisee stood alone and prayed, 'God, I thank you that I am not like other people who steal, cheat, or take part in adultery, or even like this tax collector. I give up eating twice a week, and I give one tenth of everything I get!' The tax collector, standing at a distance, would not even look up to heaven. But he beat on his chest because he was so sad. He said, 'God, have mercy on me, a sinner.' I tell you, when this man went home, he was right with God, but the Pharisee was not. All who make themselves great will be made humble, but all who make themselves humble will be made great." >>>>>>>>>>>>>>>>>>>>>>>>>>>

>> Mark 7:6

Jesus answered, "Isaiah was right when he spoke about you hypocrites. He wrote. 'These people show honor to me with words, but their hearts are far from me.'" >>>>>>>>>>>>>>>>>>>>>>>>

Lots of students like to play church. You know what I mean. Remember when you were little and you played house or cowboys and Indians? Someone would usually be the mom, the baby, Geronimo, John Wayne. But you were only playing. It wasn't real.

I see students play church. They say all the right words, know all the answers to questions, and can play worship songs on the guitar. They know just enough to impress people and get Mom and Dad off their back. As I watch them, I catch the other side. I hear what they talk about and how they talk about others. How they laugh or make fun of church away from the building and how much church bores them. I see that they know what to do, but their heart isn't in it. Maybe it is you who are playing this game.

If you are, step back and ask God to become real. You might have to look for new ways to see God. But quit playing the game. God doesn't want or need empty words. He wants your heart.

## Psalm 145:18

Cecilia and Katy used to talk all the time. In junior high they spent every moment together. They were always at each other's house, on family vacations together, in the same classes, and weekend sleepovers. It was to the point that they didn't even have to ask their parents if they could go to the other's house, they just did it. Their parents never worried about them. If they didn't see them, they just assumed they were at the other one's house.

But something changed. They got to high school and things were different. Different classes and new friends started fracturing what was once a strong relationship. By the time they were juniors, they hardly spent any time together. In hindsight it all made sense. As they talked less, they grew further and further apart. The relationship between Cecilia and Katy needed constant communication. When the communication broke down, so did the relationship.

How is your relationship with God? The openness and frequency of communication have a direct effect on the strength of your relationship with Him. What is He telling you?

Continue to do those things; give your life to doing them so your progress may be seen by everyone. Be careful in your life and in your teaching. If you continue to live and teach rightly, you will save both yourself and those who listen to you. >>>>>>

Have you discovered what you are good at yet? You've probably discovered that you're gifted and talented at something. You might enjoy teaching others, studying, or playing music. There is no doubt that there are things in your life that highly interest you and that you are good at. Maybe what you like and are good at doesn't qualify as a "spiritual gift"—it doesn't make one of the several lists of "spiritual gifts."

Don't worry if it isn't on the list. If you are using your talent for God and teaching people about who Jesus is, that is a spiritual gift. The issue now isn't whether it is a gift listed in the Bible. The issue is whether or not you are using those God-given abilities for God or letting them waste away. The gifts that you have can bring people into the kingdom of God—if you use them! How are you using those gifts which God has given you? Are you using them for Him, or just you?

Jesus went into the Temple and began to throw out the people who were selling things there. He said, "It is written in the Scriptures, 'My Temple will be a house for prayer.' But you have changed it into a 'hideout for robbers'!" >>>>>>>>>>>>>>>

It's okay to be angry, right? Look at Jesus, He got mad when He was in the temple. He started trashing the place, throwing everyone out and yelling at them. If you look closely, though, you will see a couple of the principles that Jesus used when He got angry.

First—Jesus only got angry for reasons that appeared to be an injustice to others. The Temple wasn't being used for the reason God wanted, so Jesus let the people know that.

Second—Jesus got mad at what was worth getting mad at. He didn't get angry at personal offenses against Him. He got mad when others were not treated right. People were mean to Jesus and He just let it roll, but when those same people were mean to others, Jesus did what He could, even if it meant getting angry.

What makes you mad? Do you think everything and everyone is against you, or do you get defensive for those who can't defend themselves?

## >> 1 Corinthians 13:1-2

I may speak in different languages of people or even angels. But if I do not have love, I am only a noisy bell or a crashing cymbal. I may have the gift of prophecy. I may understand all the secret things of God and have all knowledge, and I may have faith so great I can move mountains. But even with all these things, if I do not have love, then I am nothing. >>>>>>>>>>>

Trevor had every kind of Christian trinket known to man. He had a wristband showing how much he prayed, socks to remind him to walk with God, mittens for the work his hands would do for God, a fish emblem for his car, and a fish earring to remind him to always listen to God. He had it all. There was no way people could miss the fact that he was a Christian. He was a walking billboard for the franchise "Jesus Is Us."

The only thing that Trevor lacked was a genuine love for people who didn't believe the way he did. Trevor liked to argue and debate and show all the falsehoods of any belief contrary to Christianity. He enjoyed watching them fall flat on their face, not being able to argue back at him. Trevor was trying to humiliate them, and they knew it.

It doesn't matter how much Christian paraphernalia we wear. If we don't love those people we are trying to reach, it will result in us having some cool stuff and nothing more.

Good people will be glad when they see him get even. They will wash their feet in the blood of the wicked. Then people will say, "There really are rewards for doing what is right. There really is a God who judges the world." > > > > > > > > > > > >

Have you ever wondered if it is all worth it? You know what I mean—is this whole Christian life worth all the work it takes to live it? Sometimes it gets really hard. You get made fun of because people think what you believe is a crutch or just stupid. They put you down because you don't want to go out and party. It gets so intense that sometimes, when somebody starts the bashing, you just want to yell, "Shut up!" You want to show them that one day they'll get theirs.

People make you so mad sometimes that you can hardly stand it. But remember, God is the One who will deal with them, and He will. Until they stand before Him, we are called to love them and do whatever we can to show them what the kingdom of God is like.

You handle your end of dealing with these types of people and let God handle His end.

## >> Romans 12:9a

Love does not equal romance and romance does not equal love.
There is a fundamental difference in how guys and girls view dating
relationships. A girl will look for the guy to be romantic, and if he is,
she thinks, "Maybe he loves me." At the same time, girls might think
that if he isn't romantic he is only interested in himself and not her.
It all comes down to expectations. If you're in a relationship right now,
ask your boy/girlfriend what it means to be romantic. I think you will
find that a guy's definition of romance will be different from a girl's,
and that's okay. The most important thing is to keep the other person
informed. If they do something you don't like and you don't tell them,
it can be disastrous. Always think about the other person, and don't
keep score when they mess up.

Remember, just because someone is romantic doesn't mean they're
in love. And if they aren't romantic, that doesn't mean they aren't. We
are all different and see things in different ways.

When people sin, they earn what sin pays—death. But God gives us a free gift—life forever in Christ Jesus our Lord. >>>>>>>>>>>>>>>>>>>>>>

## >> Romans 6:23

Brian liked the bookends he bought. He painted one word on each bookend. On one he put the word "God" and on the other he put the word "me." He used the bookends as a place to put his Bible, and as a reminder that he is separated from God. It is Jesus that joins us to God—his Bible represented Jesus.

Brian found it sobering to look at the bookends without his Bible in the middle of them. It always reminded him that sin is what separates us from God. If not confessed, the gap will never get bridged. And that would mean separation from God forever.

We need Jesus. He brings us to where God is. The sin in our life is what keeps us from getting closer to God. We need to eliminate the sin from our life, but that sometimes feels next to impossible. We have to try and keep asking God to help us in our struggles. We want to win in our struggle over sin, not just play in the game.

Don't look for ways to separate yourself from God. Let Jesus bring you close to Him.

> Together you are the body of Christ, and each one of you is a part of that body. »»»»»»»»»

## »» 1 Corinthians 12:27

God doesn't need you, your church doesn't need you, your family doesn't need you, nor do your friends need you. Doesn't that make you feel good inside? Probably not, but think about it, God doesn't need us, yet He chooses to keep us.

There are lots of things that handicap people. But the fact is that a person can still perform very well in life with limited resources. Someone deaf can accomplish as much in life as someone with the ability to hear. The only difference is that their body is not working at its full ability.

The same is true in ministry. Ministry can and will happen without you. But in order for everyone to enjoy all of the benefits of building God's kingdom, everyone in the kingdom should be involved. So the issue is not being needed, but *wanted*. Yeah, yeah, God may not need you. But He really does *want* you. Now, how much do you want to be involved? The next step is up to you.

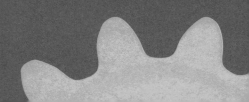

"Being a Christian is tough because of all the rules you have to follow." This is a common phrase I hear in student ministry. Many people are not interested in the claims of Christ because of the so-called rules that go along with being a Christian. So you might convince yourself that you really don't have to follow any rules when you are a Christian. The only rule that matters is to love God and love people. We can make it this fruity experience that takes no work. We expect God to be cool with anything that we do simply because He digs us no matter what. Here is the problem with that kind of thinking: Just because God loves us unconditionally does not mean we have the freedom to do as we please.

God gives very specific guidelines for our lives as believers in Him. Things like no pre-marital sex, obey the laws of the land, and love all people more than yourself. When you look at the Bible, it says that if you follow what God says, people will see that you know God.

So how are you doing? Are you following God's ways or your own? Who does your lifestyle say you know better: God or yourself?

129

## >> Matthew 14:26

What scares you and how do you handle it? It seems like everyone is scared by something different. You might not like haunted houses because of an experience you had at one when you were a kid. The ghost jumped out at you from the dark, and you were so terrified you wet your pants. It might still bother you, and if you get scared with any liquid in your bladder, it could be out before the word "Boo" is finished.

The issue usually isn't the fear itself, it is how you deal with it. There are various ways people react: throw up, get diarrhea, upset stomach, speechless, or find somewhere to hide. No matter what happens in your life, there will always be something you fear. It might be the fear of speaking in front of your class, the fear of dying, of being left out of your friends' plans, or the fear of your parents splitting up. Whatever it is, you need to ask God for help. Look at the disciples in this passage. They got freaked out when they saw someone walking on the water. When they cried out, Jesus reached out and spoke to them. What do you do when you get scared? How do you ask God for help?

> I ask that you give me an obedient heart so I can rule the people in the right way and will know the difference between right and wrong. Otherwise, it is impossible to rule this great people of yours.

## >> 1 Kings 3:9

>>>>>>>>>>>>>>>>>>>>>>>>>>>

The pressure, at times, felt unbearable to Monica. Parents and teachers had some pretty grand expectations for her and where they wanted her to go to college. Why wouldn't they—she received one of the highest scores in the state on her SAT. Colleges from all over the country were offering her scholarships. All the schools were good, and Monica didn't feel she could say in her heart that one school was better than another. Everyone else had strong opinions. Mom wanted her to stay close to home, her teachers wanted her to pick a prestigious university, and friends wanted to know if there were good sororities at any of them. What Monica really wanted to do was go to cosmetology school and learn about painting fingernails, doing make-up, and cutting hair. She didn't care about the university, but how could she tell others?

One night Monica was reading in her Bible about Solomon and the choices he made. When God asked him to make a wish, he asked for wisdom. Monica asked for the same thing. She went to God for guidance. Where do you go? It might help to put a picture of a compass on your Bible, because God will direct you when you ask Him.

"He had never sinned, and he had never lied." People insulted Christ, but he did not insult them in return. Christ suffered, but he did not threaten. He let God, the One who judges rightly, take care of him. >>>>>>>>>>>>>>>>>>>>>>>>>>>>

It takes you an hour and a half to get ready for school every morning, and you're a guy. Everything has to look just right. The hair has to be messed up just the right way, clothes need wrinkles in the right spots, and the pants need to sag just enough to irritate Mom. Still, no matter how hard you try, you don't look perfect. You can thank God for zits.

You might be a girl who thinks that everything has to be the best. You buy only designer labels, have the colors to match the season, and your hair is a $400 weave. It is all good until you realize that the Goth chick, with her black lipstick and eye-shadow, is much more popular than you are.

When it comes down to it, we are not perfect, no matter how hard we try. The perfect life was reserved for only one man, and it wasn't you. No offense, but Jesus is the only one who ever lived a perfect life on this earth and you know what? That's okay. It's okay to not be perfect, especially when you realize that you are exactly the way God wants you. There are areas to improve in, yes, but God is impressed with you because you are his creation—not because of what you wear, think, or what you can or will accomplish. Nobody's perfect. Live with it. It's okay.

But the LORD said to Samuel, "Don't look at how handsome Eliab is or how tall he is, because I have not chosen him. God does not see the same way people see. People look at the outside of a person, but the Lord looks at the heart." >>>>>>>>>

It was an event that haunted Jeremy for years. People still make fun of him for it to this day. It happened in the third grade when he went on a trip with his mom and dad. When they flew to Chicago the flight attendant gave Jeremy a set of wings to pin to his shirt. No one really noticed what the wings had written on them until he wore them to school. Everyone in his class noticed. Jeremy's wings said "future stewardess" across the bottom. The flight attendant obviously made a mistake, and Jeremy paid the price. For the next eight years his nickname became "fly girl."

Throughout the rest of his life Jeremy tried his hardest not to let it affect him, but it did. He tried hard to show that he was a real man by doing the things he thought real men did: ride motorcycles, hunt, fish, play football, and try to grow a beard. Then he realized that there were girls who liked to do many of those same things (okay, maybe not grow a beard!). It made him confused about gender roles until he realized that to God it didn't matter what he was on the outside. God cares about the heart, not looks or what you're trying not to be. What does God see when He looks at your heart?

## >> Revelation 4:34

The One who sat on the throne looked like precious stones . . . All around the throne was a rainbow the color of an emerald. Around the throne there were twenty-four other thrones with twenty-four elders sitting on them. They were dressed in white and had golden crowns on their heads. >>>>>>>

Take some time to imagine that.

Close your eyes and picture what it would be like to be there. Read on to see what the rest of the chapter (Rev. 4) has to say.

"Food is for the stomach, and the stomach for food," but God will destroy them both. The body is not for sexual sin but for the Lord, and the Lord is for the body. >>>>>>>>>>>>>>>>>>>>>>

It is so easy to do, but it always feels so wrong. It takes no time at all to get on the computer, after you make sure no one is home, and go to the sites you want to see. Beautiful women or men wearing nothing at all and doing all sorts of stuff that you never thought was humanly possible. It started by accident, but now it's a habit. Your friends are giving you sites to check out. You start to feel out of control, but don't want to tell anyone. The shame and humiliation are more than you can bear, so you say nothing.

The guilt gets so bad that you can't sleep at night. You know better than to look at that kind of stuff—they've been talking about the problem at church—but you still do. Finally you decide that you need to do something, so you ask your mom to buy a blocking program for the computer. You tell her that there is a big temptation. When she asks if you want to talk about it, you say no, but you know you can go to her if you need to.

The first defense against porn is to protect your mind. Get a filter that keeps the sites out of your house. When you go to a friend's house and they want to look at the stuff, you're going to have to make some decisions. What does God want for you?

"Then the King will say to those on his left, 'Go away from me. You will be punished. Go into the fire that burns forever that was prepared for the devil and his angels.'" >>>>>>>>>>>>>>>

Go to hell! How often have you heard that? How often have you said it?

Some people like to think of it as an eternal party, which it isn't. The truth is that hell will keep you isolated from seeing anybody. Some people think that because God is loving He can't send anyone to hell. But the truth is He's also just. He hates sin and will punish it. The only way to get out of that punishment is to claim the perfect record Jesus offers you.

Hell is a real place—one you probably don't even want to think about, much less go to. 'Cause once you're there, there's no getting out. That's why Jesus spoke more about what hell was like than what heaven is like. Make sure you end up in heaven and take everyone you know with you.

Elijah approached the people and said, "How long will you not decide between two choices? If the Lord is the true God, follow him, but if Baal is the true God, follow him!" But the people said nothing.

>>>>>>>>>>>>>>>>>>>>>>>>>>>>>>>

Options, options, options. We like to keep our options open all the time. Just in case we get sick of something, we like to have options. *TRL* has become so popular because you have options every day for what you think is the best video. When you get sick of one, you can choose a new one the next day.

Maybe you are going through your life thinking that you are young and you always need to keep all your options open. You will have time for God when you get older, but right now choosing to follow God fully would be limiting your options. You know following God is the right choice, but making Him the Lord of your life will require you to give up some of the things you like. Things that are directly contrary to God's plan for you.

So, what are you going to do? Like it or not, sooner or later, you are going to have to make the choice. I hope you will choose to completely follow God. It is a good decision to make. And here is something that might surprise you: When you choose God fully, a lot more options become available.

> "I the LORD do not change. So you descendants of Jacob have not been destroyed." >>>>>>>>>

## >> Malachi 3:6

Styles change. Remember the eighties and those funky clothes? Moods change. Just watch your best friends when they don't get something they want. Time changes. Sometimes faster than we like it to. Hopefully your underwear changes; if not, you have some issues. Jobs might change as you get offers elsewhere or just fed up with where you are. Light bulbs change—we don't like to sit in the dark too much. Boy/girlfriends change, with some people a lot more often than others.

Have you ever wondered if God changes? Take the role of women in the church. As the years have gone on, their role has increased in our churches. That is not God changing. That is the church and His people changing. God doesn't change. And that is a good thing. If He changed His mind, think of what that could mean! He could decide against heaven for anyone, kicking out those who are already there. He could judge us one way now, and a different way later. He could do with us whatever He liked and that might be good, or it might not. Thankfully He doesn't change, and He never will. To get closer to God, however, we might have to change. Think about what you need to change in your life.

Then the men were able to see. But Jesus warned them strongly, saying, "Don't tell anyone about this." But the blind men left and spread the news about Jesus all around that area. > > > > > > > > > > > >

Life was looking up for Tom. He met Heidi last year at school and thought she was pretty hot. He really liked her, the way she looked, and the group of friends she hung out with. The only thing Tom didn't like about Heidi was her boyfriend. Not that her boyfriend was a bad guy, he was actually pretty cool. But he was dating Heidi and Tom wasn't. At last his chance had come. Heidi's boyfriend gave her the "I-just-want-to-be-friends" line, and it was a pretty nice break up. Now it was Tom's turn.

Tom asked her out about two weeks after the break up and Heidi said yes. They did a lot of stuff together, but never with anyone else. Heidi wanted to keep the relationship under wraps because she didn't want to make her old boyfriend mad.

Tom couldn't contain himself, though, and told everyone. He felt like Heidi was worth bragging about, and he did. Heidi wanted to be mad, but instead she was flattered.

When good things happen in our life, it is okay to share them with others. Sometimes we need to 'show off' God in our lives. Most of the time we try to hide Him. Have you ever shown off God in your life? If not, how can you?

## ›› Ephesians 4:15

Do people who constantly change their minds drive you nuts? The type of people that change their opinion based on which group they are hanging around? You can't believe how quickly and easily they can switch gears. When they are around their Christian friends, they will be a vocal supporter of a baby's right to live as opposed to being aborted. Then, when they move to a group of friends who don't agree with the pro-life point of view, they will suddenly say that an abortion under the right circumstances is okay. The issue doesn't have to be abortion— whatever the topic, they switch their opinion to suit the group.

Sometimes you want to shake them and ask them if they actually have an opinion or if they just accept what everyone else thinks! We all need to learn how to speak the truth. It's okay to have your own opinions. They should be well thought out and based on God's Word. Use them to your advantage. Let people know they can count on you— that you mean what you say, and that you will be consistent. Make your word your bond.

## >> Genesis 2:1-3

So the sky, the earth, and all that filled them were finished. By the seventh day God finished the work he had been doing, so he rested from all his work. God blessed the seventh day and made it a holy day, because on that day he rested from all the work he had done in creating the world >>>>>>>>>

Do you enjoy taking a break?

Most everyone does. What do you do when you take a break? Some read a magazine, some take a nap, and others will use the time to talk about anything besides what they are working on. Regardless of what you do during your breaks, taking them is important. To take a rest and refresh yourself does your mind and body good. It allows you to reflect on what you have recently accomplished, think about what you want to do in the future, or just forget about what needs to be done, at least for a moment. When you find yourself getting too busy, pick an appropriate time and go ahead, take a break. (If you plan on doing it at work, please check with your boss first so you aren't given a permanent break.)

Don't get so busy in life that you can't sit back and relax . At some point you need to enjoy what you've done. God, after creating the whole world, took a break. Why don't you?

Then Jesus went up on a mountain and called to him the men he wanted, and they came to him. Jesus chose twelve men and called them apostles. He wanted them to be with him . >>>>>>>>

You are pretty psyched about what has happened. Out of the blue, your youth pastor has approached you about being discipled by him. You are excited because you have wanted to dive deeper into spiritual things, and this will give you the opportunity. The time is set up and you show up with your Bible in hand. You also bring a few devotional books that you suggest going through together. Your pastor looks over your books and says they look nice and then proceeds to just talk for the next hour. You walk away feeling a little empty. The next week you meet and he drives you with him to the mall. He has some errands to run and you get to tag along. He introduces you to some people he runs into, and you watch as he ministers to some hurting people who need him. But no Bible is ever used in your meeting.

The next week you finally ask him what is going on!? He seems a little surprised at your question. He tells you that discipleship isn't just a Bible study. That can be part of it, but it is mostly life lessons. Learning to become more like Jesus.

Look at this passage in Mark—what is the main priority to Jesus? It is, first and foremost, spending time together. What is your expectation of discipleship and how does it line up with God's word?

>> i Timothy 6:9

Those who want to become rich bring temptation to themselves and are caught in a trap. They want many foolish and harmful things that ruin and destroy people. >>>>>>>>>>>>>>>>>>>>>

How badly do you want to be rich? Wouldn't it be nice to be able to do whatever you want, whenever you want to do it? If money were never an issue, think of how happy you might be. Or would you really be happy? Lots of questions to think about. There isn't anyone who wouldn't enjoy having a little more money, or maybe a lot more money. But if we get the money, do we want the baggage that goes along with it? Remember, money doesn't buy you happiness. Have you ever heard of a guy named Howard Hughes? (If not, look him up.) He died one of the richest men in the world. He also died a recluse who wanted nothing to do with people. He was rich and he was miserable.

Usually, when people become rich, they are still not satisfied. The money they get is never enough. They always want more. Even if they have so much money they could never spend all of it in five lifetimes! Getting money becomes the obsession and everything else takes second place.

It is not wrong to have money, or even lots of money, but our only obsession in life should be God and God alone. What are you obsessed with?

## >> Luke 14:11

It might be the hardest thing to have in your life. Some people can't have it and many others don't want to have it. There are those who appear to have it, but you know they are faking their way through it. Most people who live with it are seen as nice people, but not very popular. Almost everyone believes that to get anywhere in life, you can't have it. Not everyone is good at accepting it because it makes us feel awkward. When it happens to you, you often don't expect it or it happens at the wrong time. People can sometimes feel bad for you when they see you get it. Your mom and dad probably think that you need a little more of it. Your football or volleyball coach thinks you need a lot less of it. Jesus had it and got crucified for it. It would have saved Adam, Eve, and Moses had they been a little more in tune with it. In it's absence, we may not have any close friends. With it, you could change the world, or at least your corner of it. Do you have it? Have you figured out what it is yet? Get it.

## >> Genesis 37:3-4

Since Joseph was born when his father Israel was old, Israel loved him more than his other sons. He made Joseph a special robe with long sleeves. When Joseph's brothers saw that their father loved him more than he loved them, they hated their brother and could not speak to him politely. >>>>>>>

If there is one person in this world that irritates you more than anyone, it is your little sister. Mom and Dad are always giving her what she wants. You have to scrape and beg for anything you get, usually having to pay for it out of your own pocket. When you turned thirteen you got fifty dollars from your parents to put toward a new bike. When your sister turned thirteen, they bought her a new bike! It was seven months past your sixteenth birthday before your parents let you drive by yourself. Your sister got a key to the car on her sixteenth birthday and drove to school the next day.

Your sister has done nothing to you. You are irritated because she gets everything from your parents. Think about this: Maybe your parents are so generous to her because you have shown that you can be reliable. You paved the way for her. Maybe it helps, maybe it doesn't, but remember this: she will be your sister the rest of your life. In about ten years she might even be one of your best friends. Treat her well now, and it will pay off later.

## ⟩⟩ Psalm 23: 1-3a

Feeling tired or worn out? Rest. Let God take care of you. Just hang with Him for a while.

It was not an enemy insulting me. I could stand that. It was not someone who hated me. I could hide from him. But it is you, a person like me, my companion and good friend. We had a good friendship and walked together to God's Temple.

>>>>>>>>>>>>>>>>>>>>>>>>>>>>

Derek and Devon were inseparable.

They did everything together: classes, sports, Nintendo, getting in trouble. One night the two of them were bored and just hanging out. They got the idea that it would be fun to go throw some eggs at houses around the neighborhood. They grabbed a dozen eggs out of the refrigerator and took off. They tossed 'em and then ran home, thinking nobody saw them in the dark. But one of the neighbors did. Devon denied doing anything— he was at home doing homework, but said he did know that Derek was out throwing eggs. Derek got in all the trouble and Devon was praised for being so honest. Derek ended up having to clean up the entire mess and apologize to all the neighbors. He tried to tell everyone that Devon helped, but the words fell on deaf ears.

What would you do? Try to just let it go? Take revenge? You are guilty, so own up to your mistake. Devon has to live with what he did. Let God deal with him.

Let us think about each other and help each other to show love and do good deeds. » » » » » » » »

## >> Hebrews 10:24

Read the verse again. What are some ways that you can show love to people around you? Not goofy, dorky, or even sexy love, but love that puts the other person first. Once you start thinking about what you can do for other people, and actually do it, your love for them will automatically increase. If you take it upon yourself to encourage and help the people around you, they'll catch a glimpse of how they're supposed to live. They may never understand how to do it until they see someone else doing it. So make it happen. Take the rest of this page and write down people who need your help and how you can make it happen.

Always be humble, gentle, and patient, accepting each other in love. > > > > > > > > > > > > > >

## >> Ephesians 4:2

Evie has been planning this special night for her boyfriend for a while. She wants to get beyond the "movie and pizza" rut they are currently caught in. So she plans a candlelight dinner on a downtown rooftop for her and Will. Her friends are helping out. It'll be a surprise to Will, and everyone will be in on making the night a success.

So, the night comes and it turns out to be a disaster. Most of Evie's friends forget and never show up to help. The two that do show forget to bring the food. Evie had checked with the building owner for permission, but they forgot to tell the security company. They come on the scene and cause a big stir. After they settle the mix-up, pigeons start descending on the place and make the rooftop miserable. Evie and Will finally finish the evening at a fast food restaurant, laughing about how it all turned out.

They talk for hours and when Evie gets home she realizes that the night really wasn't a disaster. She got to know Will better because of the time they spent laughing and talking. Shouldn't that be the goal in dating anyway? Simply getting to know the other person better and putting their needs before your own?

"But I say to you, love your enemies. Pray for those who hurt you." >>>>>>>>>>>>>>>>>>>

You did try to be nice. It just wasn't working out as far as you were concerned. So you broke up with him, letting both of you get on with your lives. Then the problems started. When you would get in your car after work, you would see his car out in the distance and see him watching you. You went to his house once to try and talk with him, but it just turned into a huge fight. You got so desperate you told him that you were seeing someone else. It wasn't true, but you just wanted him to leave you alone. He ended up throwing a cup at you and calling you a slut. And that was one of the nicer things he said to you.

Now the rumors are flying—and you're sure they're from him. Stuff like you wouldn't "put out" so he dumped you. It hurts. You never had sex with him; in fact, it never was an issue in your relationship. So what do you do?

This might sound silly, but it's not. Pray for him. Every other option seems to fail. It's time to turn it over to God and let Him take care of it. It will only be by God's help that you will get over your anger and forgive him.

Understanding is like a fountain which gives life to those who use it, but foolishness brings punishment to fools. >>>>>>>>>>>>>>>>>>>>>>>

It was one of the most embarrassing moments in Kevin's life. He was out on a date with Pam, and he walked her up to the door at the end of the evening. Okay, so it was the first date, but they had had a good time and he thought a goodnight kiss was in order. As he turned his head in order to plant one on her, she looked at him and, well, yelled, "What are you doing?!"

"I'm giving you a kiss goodnight."

Pam came back with, "Not on these lips!" and walked into her house.

Ouch, that hurt. And Kevin had thought the date went well. He called Pam the next day and asked why she didn't have a good time. She said she did, she just doesn't kiss on the first date. She only kisses guys she has a commitment with.

Assumptions can hurt us if we are not careful. Don't assume. We don't always know what the other person is thinking. Always communicate to play it safe. If you think that a kiss might be in order, ask first. It will blow the girl away.

"But it should not be that way among you. Whoever wants to become great among you must serve the rest of you like a servant." >>>>>>>>>>

Life is good for Charity, just ask her. Better yet, just wait, she'll tell you. Charity has a little issue with her ego. Okay, a big issue—mainly because it is such a big ego. She never lifts a finger to help anyone else, but is quick to demand that other people help her whenever she needs it. When she gets a new car, which seems to be every other month, she lets everyone know. If you tell her that she looks nice her reply is "I know." It drives you crazy. How can someone with such nice parents be such a butt? She always points out the flaws in your life, and then she makes sure that she tells everyone about them.

She thinks it is incredibly tacky that you volunteer once a week in a soup kitchen, helping people who are a little less fortunate. "Those people are there because they want to be there, serving them soup does no good," she says to you. It breaks your heart, and she is not the only person out there who thinks that way.

Egos left unchecked will destroy people. There are a few good things about people with big egos. First, they help us see how good it is to help others. Second, they show us specific ways we shouldn't live our lives.

You have no doubt heard the saying "Beauty is only skin deep." It's worth memorizing. There probably isn't any person in the world that doesn't wish that they were just a little better looking than they are. In every ad you see the people all look perfect. You realize that there is no way in the world you will ever measure up to those kinds of looks. The truth is nobody is perfect, just ask 'em. Every model or actor could tell you their imperfections.

Guess what is going to happen one day? Styles are going to change. What was attractive in high school will turn tacky in a couple of years, guaranteed. And that's okay. Our lives shouldn't be wrapped up in what we look like. Looks won't bring you contentment. They might make you feel good for a moment, but true happiness will only be found in Jesus. You can put your trust in what you look like to get you through life, and eventually you'll be let down. If you trust in the Lord to get you through life, you never will be let down.

How much time do you put into your looks as opposed to your spiritual life?

Nobody wants the reputation of being a bad date. If you get labeled a bad date, you probably won't date at all. At best your dating days are limited. Being a good date requires you to follow four simple rules. They are as follows:

*Never assume.* Always know where you stand and where you are going. Don't assume you'll have a second date unless you've talked about it.

*Keep your word.* If you say you are going to call tomorrow, call tomorrow. If you don't see the relationship going anywhere, let them know, but be gentle. They may be thinking the opposite.

*Be creative.* There are only so many good movies on in a given month—nobody likes boring dates or dates that get caught in a rut. It might take some thinking, but it will pay off. If you're creative, you'll always have someone who wants to go out with you.

*Treat each date like they are going to marry your best friend someday.* Think about it, if they married your best friend, you would be glad you treated them right! You hope your future spouse is being treated well, don't you?

These are not the only rules, but they'll help you on the finer points of dating. Do it right.

The LORD says, "So I will teach those who make idols. This time I will teach them about my power and my strength. Then they will know that my name is the LORD." >>>>>>>>>>>>>>>>>>>>>>>>

>> Jeremiah 16:21

"It just makes this whole world, or at least my corner, easier to deal with," thinks Susan. Susan really wants everyone she knows and loves to end up in heaven. She wants to believe that if they are good people and never go to jail or anything like that, they will end up in eternity with her regardless of what they've done with Jesus. Susan wants to believe this because she doesn't want to bug her friends or have them think she's a freak. It is so much easier to believe that a God of love and understanding would gladly open the doors to His kingdom to all those who deserve it.

The thing is, no one deserves it—not on their own, at least. Only people who acknowledge God as King and their need of Jesus as a Savior will be on the reservation list in heaven. It isn't unfair, it is simply the way God set it up. No matter how hard someone tries, how good they are, or how much they give, they can't enter heaven without acknowledging the death and resurrection of Jesus. Then they have to know that they need the work of Jesus to restore their relationship with God.

It is better for them to think you are a freak and know the truth, than to think you are totally cool and end up in hell for eternity.

## >> Revelation 21:3-4

And I heard a loud voice from the throne, saying, "Now God's presence is with people, and he will live with them, and they will be his people. God himself will be with them and will be their God. He will wipe away every tear from their eyes, and there will be no more death, sadness, crying, or pain, because all the old ways are gone." >>>>

It is actually better than you can imagine. We can imagine a whole lot of great things when it comes to our thoughts of heaven, but believe it or not, heaven will be better than our best thoughts. It might be weird to think that, as a Christian, we'll spend eternity in one place, and that one place will be so cool that we will never get bored. In fact, when we get to heaven, boring probably won't ever be in our vocabulary. We won't know the meaning of the word.

Think about the most amazing time of worship you have ever experienced. A time when you were so caught up in the moment of surrender to God that you didn't want to quit or move on. You wanted to stay there. It was a unique moment of true worship. That is what heaven will be like—a total experience in the presence of God. He will reserve His best stuff for us when we get there. Make sure that you get as many people as you can to go with you.

"Can you understand the secrets of God? Can you search the limits of the Almighty? His limits are higher than the heavens; you cannot reach them! They are deeper than the grave; you cannot understand them!" >>>>>>>>>>>>>>>>

Sometimes we wonder if we can really know God. God is so big and vast while we are so little and feeble. Can we really understand Him?

It is kind of like our parents. We spend a lot of time with them—at one point our lives were completely dependent on them. Then we get to our teenage years and wonder, "Who are these people?" It's like we all of a sudden wake up and wonder if we ever really knew them or if we ever will.

But here's the real issue. There is a difference between knowing God and knowing about God.

There is much about God that we don't know. There are things we do know about God that we can't understand. That is okay, because even though we don't know everything about God, we can know Him. We don't need to know everything about a person to start a great relationship with them. As the relationship develops, so does our understanding of the person. It's the same with God.

Get to know God better and you will begin to understand Him more fully.

>> John 13:14-15

If I, your Lord and Teacher, have washed your feet, you also should wash each other's feet. I did this as an example so that you should do as I have done for you. >>>>>>>>>>>>>>>>>>>>>>>>>

Joey sat there listening to the latest spiel from his youth pastor. They were getting the talk about serving one another. It was a good talk, but it wasn't applying to him. For years Joey had stacked chairs for the custodians at church, served meals to the homeless, and put toy packages together for the local Crisis Pregnancy Center. It wasn't something he really needed to hear, and he was bored.

As Joey was daydreaming, he overheard something. Foot washing. Joey liked to help people but come on, taking off smelly socks, touching feet, and washing them off wasn't serving—it was gross!

"Foot washing was something that they did back in the old days, when Jesus walked the earth, but it isn't necessary today," Joey thought. How could he politely excuse himself and get out of doing this?

Nothing came to mind, so Joey sucked it up and took part. As he was washing the feet of the person next to him, all he could think was "Not only is this gross, it's humiliating." Then it clicked. Sometimes we need a little humility to understand what service and sacrifice are all about. If you want to learn sacrificial service with a dose of humility mixed in, try washing someone's feet. It is a great experience and a valuable lesson.

They fight and fight and fight. You just wish it would all end. But when they tell you that it's over, you're devastated. You run to the bathroom and throw up. Your mom comes in and hugs you while you cry. "Why do you have to get divorced?" you yell at her. "Can't you be grown-ups and work this out? It's so stupid!"

But they've decided. It's over and Dad's moving out tomorrow. And you've got to decide where you want to live. Obviously the answer is "Here, with both of you." But it's just not going to happen. How in the world are you ever going to decide? Either way you're going to miss one of them really, really badly. And you feel guilty having to pick one. You tell them you want to leave it to them, and the fights start again. "Fine," you say, "I'll decide."

A week later you've decided. You're going to stick with Mom, but your brother's going with Dad. You cry and cry and cry every night. You have a hard time sleeping. School is awful—you haven't told your friends yet.

What do you do? 1. Tell some friends—you really need their love and prayers right now. 2. Don't let Satan convince you that you should feel guilty. This has nothing to do with you; it's your parents' decision. 3. Love both your parents and be supportive of them. They're trying to deal with the marriage ending plus not getting to live with their kids anymore. 4. Pray—all the time. God does care.

Fathers, do not make your children angry, but raise them with the training and teaching of the Lord.

>>>>>>>>>>>>>>>>>>>>>>>>>>>>>>>

It was bad enough that she did it to you. Now you are noticing the same tendencies toward your little sister as she is getting older.

It started with a few "put downs" from your mom. After that, she wanted to prove to you that she could control you. So she forced you to only wear clothes that she approved of. It then escalated to her slapping you when she didn't approve of your actions. Before you knew it, she wasn't approving of anything—and instead of slapping you, she burned you with her cigarette. If a smoke wasn't handy, she would beat (not spank) you with anything she could get her hands on. It happened to you for years, and you tried to prove you could take it. But now she is starting in on your little sister. You can't sit by and watch it happen. One day, you come home and see your younger sister crying. You see the bruises. She tells you it was Mom. That's it, you're ready to deal with her yourself.

It might seem like the right thing to do, but it's not. Your mom needs professional help. If your parents are abusing you, talk with an adult you can trust. Don't let it go, hoping it will go away. And don't try to prove you can "take it." Call this number for help: 1-800-4-A-CHILD.

## >> Matthew 16:24-25

Then Jesus said to his followers, "If people want to follow me, they must give up the things they want. They must be willing even to give up their lives to follow me. Those who want to save their lives will give up true life, and those who give up their lives for me will have true life." >>>>>>>>>>>>

Everything has a price. Nothing is free. People might tempt you with free offers, like software or vacations, but there will be a catch. For example, the software is great, but it only works on their new operating system that you will need to go out and buy. Vacations for free are nice, but you usually have to spend a day listening to a sales pitch about a new condo or something like that. It would be nice if things didn't come with a cost, but they always do. It might not cost you money—it might cost your attitude or maybe even your happiness.

Jesus told us that to truly follow Him, it would cost us. Maybe a lot of money that we might feel compelled to give up, maybe friends who reject us because of what we believe, or maybe even our lives. There are always costs to following Jesus. What are you willing to give Him and give up for Him? Take some time and look in your Bible to see all that Jesus gives you and gave up for you.

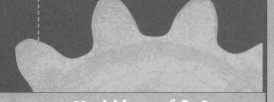

Then he said, "I tell you the truth, you must change and become like little children. Otherwise, you will never enter the kingdom of heaven." >>>>>>>

## >> Matthew 18:3

What do you change a lot? Clothes. Haircuts. E-mail addresses. College majors. Your mind.

One of the hardest things to quickly change in our life is our attitude. We sometimes get so entrenched in what we feel that we are not only unwilling, but unable to change the way we respond. It is noticeable to everyone around us that our attitude bites, but we don't want to swallow our pride and admit it. So we leave it alone, making everyone around us uncomfortable.

An easy way to change your attitude is to think like a little kid. Don't make everything so complicated, keep it simple. We make life too hard sometimes and our attitude starts to slip into the toilet. Think with more simplicity and lighten up. You won't always get your way in life, and that's okay—you shouldn't expect to. Think like a kid.

>> Micah 1:3-4

See, the LORD is coming out of his place; he is coming down to walk on the tops of the mountains. The mountains will melt under him, and the valleys will crack open, like wax near a fire, like water running down a hillside. > > > > > > > > > > > > >

Can you picture that? God is amazingly powerful. Think about him today. Talk to him. Isn't it cool that you get to talk to God—just the two of you?!?

163

"Listen to me: a time is coming when you will be scattered, each to his own home. That time is now here. You will leave me alone, but I am never really alone, because the Father is with me." >>>>>

The day was here, and Ryan was a little bummed. He knew it was going to be a hard year. Natalie, his girlfriend for the last two years, was heading off to college six hundred miles away. She was a year older, so he still had a year left in high school. This was not cool. All of Ryan's friends were the same class as Natalie. He liked hanging out with the older group and didn't have a lot of friends in his own class.

He thought about this verse in Matthew where Jesus talked about knowing when He would be alone, yet He knew God would always be with Him. So Ryan tried to remember that, no matter how lonely he felt, God was with him. Then Ryan made a concentrated effort to not get lonely. He worked on some old friendships. He treated the people around him like they were close, trusted friends. And Ryan looked in the mirror and asked, "Am I a good friend to the people around me?"

Ryan did okay his senior year. As a matter of fact, it was a great year, as Ryan learned that with God we are never alone. Now he is looking at taking these same principles to college with him, leaving friends and family again.

Because we must all stand before Christ to be judged. Each of us will receive what we should get—good or bad—for the things we did in the earthly body. >>>>>>>>>>>>>>>>>>>>>>>

No way around it, none at all. I wish there were, to tell you the truth, but the Bible makes it clear. There is no way to avoid it. We will all stand before Christ to be judged for everything that we have done in our life. Think about it. Everything in your life that you have done, good and bad, will be brought up for examination in front of Jesus. The thought of it should literally scare you. Without our relationship with Jesus we would be destined to an eternity without Him.

Everything comes out before Him. That piece of candy you stole from the store when you were five, that lie you told yesterday, all of it. But the good news is that all the good things will be brought up as well. Mowing your grandma's lawn, helping out at school, it's all there.

It makes you think about your life and what you have done. If there were a scale that weighed your life between good deeds and bad deeds, which way would it tip? Find one of those old scales and put it in your room—let it remind you of where the weight of deeds in your life is falling.

## >> Matthew 27:30

Why would he do it? Why would Jesus allow himself to be beaten? Why would He allow Himself to be spat on? Why would He go through the humiliation of having people publicly make fun of Him? Why would he sit quietly as insults and lies were being said about Him? Why would Jesus wear a crown of thorns that pierced through His skin and scratched His skull? Why would Jesus put up no protest to the treatment He was given? Why would He lay on the ground as spikes were driven through His wrists? Why didn't He call down His angels and wipe everyone out? Why did He comfort the men on the crosses beside Him when He should have been more concerned about Himself?

There are many questions that we as Christians ask when we try to understand the role Jesus plays in our relationship with God. It is not a complicated answer either. The reason why Jesus did all of these things is simple. He did it because He loves us so much that He would do what was needed to restore our relationship with God.

This is why I use stories to teach the people: They see, but they don't really see. They hear, but they don't really hear or understand. >>>>>>>>>

>> Matthew 13:13

Sometimes we just make it too hard. We try and bring some great theological truth to people who have little or no ability to understand who God is. We try to show how smart we are about God. We forget that most of the people outside of the church don't know much about God or even care about God. They may like spirituality, but God? No way.

So don't make it so difficult. Simplify what you want to say. The easiest way to do this is to tell stories. It is what Jesus did. He told stories because he knew people might not understand the plain truth in front of them. He talked about things people easily identified with: farming, shepherding, and money. People got the meaning of the story without feeling like they were being judged by Jesus.

Seems like a good plan. So, what story could you tell? Tell about your life. Tell how God is working in you and through you. Talk about what you did yesterday and how you know God is with you. Tell about what you did in church this week. Tell your story. It's easy.

But people are tempted when their own evil desire leads them away and traps them. This desire leads to sin, and then the sin grows and brings death.

>>>>>>>>>>>>>>>>>>>>>>>>>>>>>>

Five warning signs that it is lust and not love:

You know he has a girlfriend and you don't care, you still ask him out because you think he is hot.

When you think about her, you picture her naked.

You daydream about him making out with you.

All that you think about is what you'll get out of the relationship. You have no desire to put anything into it.

You don't want a relationship, you want a fling—some fun with no consequences. If it's going to turn into something you have to work at, you're gone.

If you're not careful, lust will get the better of you. It will eat at you until you start acting on your desires. It will lead to more serious problems like sex, pregnancy, STDs . . . if you don't do anything about it.

And here's the deal: Everybody deals with lust. It's not just a guy issue. Girls have the same problem. Don't let it win. Ask God to help you get control of your mind.

## >> Ephesians 6:2-3

The command says, "Honor your father and mother." This is the first command that has a promise with it—"Then everything will be well with you, and you will have a long life on the earth." >>>>>>>>

Sometimes we think our parents are the biggest dorks in the world. They aren't really, but it feels that way.

Some have rules that are so dumb—like an 8:30 curfew on the weekend!? Some want us to like everything they like. Others want to be so hip to us that our best friend is their best friend. Some are so strict that they make us feel like they never want us to grow up. Some are so easy-going it seems like they never have grown up themselves. Some give too much discipline and others don't give enough. There are lots of times that you find yourself dreaming of the day you won't have to live with them anymore, and figuring out how to manage while you still do.

It is interesting that the command in the Bible about parents is the only one that has a promise attached—in other words, a condition. If we not only obey our parents but *honor* them, God will grant us a long life. So there is a benefit to loving them.

Even though you might think they're the biggest dorks in the world, honor them. They love you and want the best for your life. Believe it or not, you sometimes don't make it so easy on them yourself.

Praise be to the God and Father of our Lord Jesus Christ. In God's great mercy he has caused us to be born again into a living hope, because Jesus Christ rose from the dead. > > > > > > > > > > > > > > >

Erin and Matt had been going out for two years when Matt started to like Angela. Matt, acting on his impulses, broke up with Erin to be fair. He thought that if he was beginning to like Angela, and not liking Erin as much, it was time to move on. To Erin, anyone would be bad for Matt to like, but Angela? Angela always thought she was God's gift to men with her big brown eyes and "fitness trainer" body.

Erin was doing okay for about a month, but it finally got to her. She started to get really depressed. Life wasn't worth it anymore. She and Matt had such big plans together, and now he was probably making those same plans with this bimbo. When Erin saw them walk down the hall hand-in-hand, she decided that she couldn't bear it anymore. That night she wrote a note telling everyone that life without Matt wasn't worth living and proceeded to down three bottles of pills from her parents' medicine chest.

When Erin woke up, she was in the hospital surrounded by her family. They let her know that over twenty of her friends were in the waiting room, really worried about her. Fortunately she would be okay.

Maybe you have had those thoughts, the ones that say "Life isn't worth living." It takes a lot to get to such a point of hopelessness that you would end your own life. Think through what you do have to live for, not what you don't. Suicide is a permanent solution to what is a temporary problem. Get help by calling this number: 1-800-SUICIDE.

People did not think it was important to have a true knowledge of God. So God left them and allowed them to have their own worthless thinking and to do things they should not do. >>>>>>>

It's Saturday night and your friends are all going out to see a movie. When you tell your parents, they ask which one. It's rated R, but you've got a great, honest relationship with your parents. You tell 'em what it is. They ask how you'll get in since you are only fifteen and you need to be seventeen to buy a ticket. "Oh, they always let us in" is your quick reply. Mom and Dad tell you they aren't crazy about it, but they leave it up to you. So you go see the movie but wish you hadn't. There were some disturbing, demonic scenes that your friends thought were cool, but gave you some weird dreams.

So what would you do differently next time? Don't see movies you aren't supposed to, unless your parents take you. I know it sounds awful, but it is a good rule of thumb to follow the rating system, even with movies you rent. Also, read the reviews and find out why the movies got rated the way they did. Discuss the ratings with your parents, and get their advice. Basically, make an intelligent decision.

There is an old saying: "Garbage in, garbage out." Honoring God has as much to do with what we let in as what we live out.

## >> 2 Corinthians 9:2

I know you want to help. I have been bragging about this to the people in Macedonia, telling them that you in Southern Greece have been ready to give since last year. And your desire to give has made most of them ready to give also. >>>>>>>>

Erika usually gets upset when she comes to the Student Ministries' events and they look cheesy. The posters around the room look like a kindergarten class drew them, the food is always stale corn chips, and the music is the greatest Christian hits of 1983. Erika finds the way the ministry works embarrassing and is glad that she doesn't ever bring any friends to the events. She would die if her friends at school came and saw where she went to church. Mike, Erika's youth pastor, has asked her to be involved, but she always finds a way to avoid it. Mike is left with no help to make the ministry what the students want.

Finally, one day Erika can't come up with an excuse to get out of helping. She comes one afternoon and helps Mike and some other students plan a worship night for the group. She finds herself excited about being involved and suddenly spear-heads a team to redecorate the room.

All it took was Erika's help. She got so involved that others are now helping out, and the ministry is improving. All it took was one person and a servant's attitude. Why don't you be the one?

**>> Ephesians 6:12**

Our fight is not against people on earth but against the rulers and authorities and the powers of this world's darkness, against the spiritual powers of evil in the heavenly world. > > > > > > > > > > > >

When you read this verse it reminds you of something you might find in a Spielberg movie. It has all the makings of a good Hollywood script. Unfortunately it is all real. There is a war going on. It is a war that we cannot see, yet we can feel its effects. It's a war that starts out for your soul, and if the enemy of God doesn't get your soul, he will satisfy himself by corrupting your life. Satan will do anything he is allowed to in order to keep you out of heaven, and if it doesn't work on you, he will try to keep your friends out. He will make you ineffective.

Sometimes, when we try our evangelism techniques, we get frustrated that everyone we talk to doesn't become a Christian. In the midst of a war, not all battles are won. Take comfort in the fact that we will win the war. But remember that Satan will not roll over and let us pull people out of hell. He will do anything he can to keep these people from hearing and understanding the truth. Fight back.

> They worshipped and thanked the Lord, saying, "He is good; his love continues forever." >>>>>>>

## >> 2 Chronicles 7:3b

Thank God for His love today. Talk with Him for awhile.
There's nothing better.

We fight with weapons that are different from those the world uses. Our weapons have power from God that can destroy the enemy's strong places. We destroy people's arguments. >>>>>>

One of my all-time favorite movies is *Braveheart*. I love the history, the story, and the epic battle scenes. When I watched it for the first time, I noticed how primitive the weapons of war were compared to today. Think of what an F-16 fighter jet could have done on the thirteenth-century battlefields of Great Britain. What would the Scots have given for one? Well, it didn't happen that way.

Wars in the physical world are fought with guns, bombs, radars, and military power. The war in the spiritual world is not fought with such obvious weapons. This war is fought with the heart and mind. If we want to win people into the kingdom of God, we have to love them and comfort them with words of encouragement. Our battle isn't to destroy our enemy—that is the job God will do. Our mission is to rescue prisoners. To free them from the bondage that they are under, living a life contrary to what God wants for them. Direct people to the freedom they can know with God by loving them and listening to them. Then let the Spirit of God do His job. Use your weapons to free prisoners, not to try to destroy the enemy.

## >> i Corinthians 10:13

The only temptation that has come to you is that which everyone has. But you can trust God, who will not permit you to be tempted more than you can stand. But when you are tempted, he will also give you a way to escape so that you will be able to stand it. >>>>>>>>>>>>>>>>>>>>>>>>

Wade and a bunch of his friends were out on a typical summer night. They were goofing off, trying to find a good place to hang out or swim. As they were driving, Chris pulled out a joint and let everyone know that as soon as the sun went down, the real fun would begin. Wade had never smoked pot in his life and he didn't want to start now, but these were his friends. He didn't want to ditch them. They stopped by the store to pick up some chips when Jodi and Dale honked at them in the parking lot. The two of them were going to a movie and asked if Wade wanted to join them. He politely declined.

About a half hour later, Wade's dad called on the cell phone to see if he wanted to eat dinner, and Wade told him that they were headed to the river to go swimming. As they all sat along the side of the river, Chris lit the joint and Wade, not wanting to look like a jerk, smoked it. He rationalized it by saying God must have wanted him to try it because He never provided a way out.

Are you looking for the escape route? Wade had at least two chances to get out, and he ignored both of them. God doesn't delight in sin, ever. Look next time.

## >> Revelation 3:19

"I correct and punish those whom I love. So be eager to do right, and change your hearts and lives." >>>>>>>>>>>>>>>>>>>>>>>>>

It isn't popular today to talk about standards, but they are important. Standards are guidelines you set up in your life to keep you from getting in a position of falling into sin. If you have no standards, you will more than likely do whatever you want with little or no regard for how it affects others or even hurts you.

I used to ask the high school guys in my discipleship group to have some simple standards. One of them was that they were not to go into their girlfriend's bedroom. Now you might think that is a little extreme, but the point was that they could get themselves into trouble if that room became too comfortable. Also, it showed the girls that they were willing to set some boundaries on the relationship, even if they never intended for anything to happen. There were plenty of other rooms in the house in which they could spend time.

So what kind of standards do you have? Will you always uphold them or will you allow them to be altered depending on who you're with? Standards are valuable to have and hold on to.

You have a saying, 'Four more months till harvest.' But I tell you, open your eyes and look at the fields ready for harvest now. >>>>>>>>>>>>>>

## >> John 4:35

Lots of people want to wait until they are older or have had their fun in high school and maybe college before they take the claims of Jesus seriously. It is a dangerous game to play. You see, in high school you have the greatest opportunity for evangelism you might *ever* have in your life. You are spending up to eight hours a day with several hundred people (depending on the size of your school) and statistics say that a good portion of them are non-Christians. You are the one that can make the difference. You don't need to wait for your youth pastor, friends, or until you're older. Make it happen now.

Waiting can ruin your credibility. Your friends will think that you are not serious about what you believe, and if you're not serious about it, why should they be?

Act today, don't wait for tomorrow. Who do you know that needs Jesus right now?

> "If anyone comes to me but loves his father, mother, wife, children, brothers, or sisters—or even life—more than me, he cannot be my follower."

## >> Luke 14:26

> > > > > > > > > > > > > > > > > > > > > > > > > > > >

Jesus made it clear what it cost to be one of his followers. Why would He put such a heavy price on us? Because He wants our total devotion to Himself. So what do we do? We put sports in front of Him. We put our girl/boyfriends in front of Him. We put our desires in front of Him. We put our car in front of Him. We put working to make money in front of Him. We may even put a missions trip in front of Jesus.

As you think about it, what do you put in front of Jesus? Is He at the forefront of your life? Is He the very essence of who you are? When people look at you or hear your name, what is the first thing they think of? That is a good measure of where Jesus stands in your life. Don't let Him slip to the back of the line. Put Him in front where He belongs.

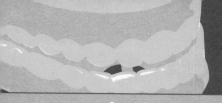

Examine and see how good the Lord is. Happy is the person who trusts him. >>>>>>>>>>>>

>> Psalm 34:8

Going to the dentist is not my favorite thing. I get there and wait in a room full of magazines that my mom loves, but I don't relate to at all. Then I get called into the back room and sit in that awkward chair. Then I need my bib, so that I don't drool all over myself. After I sit down I see all of the tools that are going to prod my mouth for some sort of decay.

Then they put this film in my mouth that is way too big and tell me to "bite down hard" while they x-ray, and I gag. My jaw starts quivering as the film gouges the side of my cheek. Now comes the fun part. Greta the Barbarian is going to get the plaque off my teeth with these spiked metal sticks. She starts scraping so hard that my gums bleed. After thirty torturous minutes of getting scraped, I get buffed. I get the grit from the buffing caught in between my teeth, and Greta shreds the floss as she tries to get it out. After the whole ordeal, something cool happens: My teeth feel great, very smooth and shiny.

Examining God might create the same type of experience. When you look at who He is and what He wants do in your life, it might hurt a little in the beginning. Like a dental exam, letting God in to clean out the crud in our life can be painful. In the end, though, you will find that He is worth it, always!

When he saw the crowds, he felt sorry for them because they were hurting and helpless, like sheep without a shepherd. >>>>>>>>>>>>>>

Do you have compassion? I mean true compassion? To the point that sometimes you can't sleep or eat because you feel the pain of others, even though nothing has happened to you?

A couple of years ago I was on a mission trip in Guatemala and visited a cerebral palsy unit of a hospital. There were around two hundred cribs in the room that housed these patients, and each held a person. The age range was anywhere from one month to twenty-five years old. I saw kids crying, in pain, and lonely. There were probably six nurses, but they couldn't handle all the kids alone. There just weren't enough caregivers. Finally, with my friend Erik beside me, we started touching these kids to try to calm them. When my hand touched their cheeks, they almost immediately stopped crying. It was amazing. To look at all these kids, many of whom were abandoned, I was crushed.

It is a good picture of what my heart needs to be for those who don't know Jesus. They sometimes simply need a touch, but I get scared to reach out. How is God working on you to create compassion for a world that generally feels abandoned?

181

>> Psalm 46:10

God says, "Be quiet and know that I am God. I will be supreme over all the nations; I will be supreme in the earth." >>>>>>>>>>>>>>>>>>>>>>>

Although I never got told to "sit down and shut up" by my parents—mainly because the phrase "shut up" was considered as bad as any cuss word in our house—I'm sure there were times when they felt like I needed to hear it. I can think of a few times in church when I got asked if I wanted to go sit out in the car, to which I replied "yes," only to have Mom thump me and say "sit still."

There are times in our lives when God probably wants to do the same thing with us. He wants to say, "Sit down and shut up." Why would He want to say that? Because sometimes, as we go through life, we get cocky enough to think that we know more than the people around us. I know I did it with my teachers. People do it with their youth pastors. It becomes a problem when we think we have a better plan than God, and we don't want to listen to Him. Sometimes He needs to get our attention, so He says, "Sit down and shut up." Why? Because He is God, and frankly, He does a much better job of being God than you or I could.

When the angels left them and went back to heaven, the shepherds said to each other, "Let's go to Bethlehem. Let's see this thing that has happened which the Lord has told us about." > > > > > > > >

A couple of years ago my mom went on a tour of Israel. She went over for a couple of weeks and had a great time, seeing many of the places where Jesus actually walked around. When she got home and was telling me about everything she did, she made the comment that Bethlehem was just this little town that wasn't very impressive to her at all. Aside from the spot where they believe Jesus was born, there wasn't anything there that captured her interest. She was a little disappointed, probably because most of her impressions of this town came from pretty cards and sweet songs at Christmas.

As I have thought about my mom's reflections, I think it is great that Jesus was born in a little podunk town like Bethlehem. What better place for the humblest of servants to enter this world than a small, nothing town like Bethlehem. No glitter, glamour, or hype, just a crusty stable and the King of Kings.

It makes me realize how unimpressed God is with what we have. He isn't into stuff. He genuinely loves *who we are*, and we need to always keep that at the front of our relationship with Him.

God did not give us a spirit that makes us afraid but a spirit of power and love and self control.

>>>>>>>>>>>>>>>>>>>>>>>>>>>>>>>>>

## >> 2 Timothy 1:7

You have decided to get involved with your Student Ministry by helping them with a mission project. In the midst of the project, you find yourself lying to anyone who asks you what you are doing. You tell them you are doing humanitarian aid or going on a trip, anything other than telling people that you are a Christian working on a mission trip. On a crowded bus in downtown Mexico City, a stranger asks you what you are doing in Mexico. You reply disinterestedly, "We're here to help some people." Your friends hear you and you see confusion in their eyes. Hey, you just don't want to have to go into the whole story. Besides, it wasn't a lie. You really are there to help people.

Truth is, you are a little nervous to let people know that you are "acting out your faith" on a mission trip. You admire the way others can freely talk about how God works in their lives, how they can't help but serve Him in return.

Remember, that feeling of timidity didn't come from God. He gives you the power to be bold with your faith. He gives you love and the ability to live a disciplined life. Which one of these four traits is evident in your life? Don't be shy. Be bold! Find ways to increase your faith. Look for new ways to love those around you. Don't sit on the sidelines—get in the game.

Being afraid of people can get you into trouble, but if you trust the Lord, you will be safe. ⟩ ⟩ ⟩ ⟩ ⟩ ⟩

## ⟩⟩ Proverbs 29:25

Once someone loses it, it can be next to impossible to get it back. It can be done, but not without a lot of work. I'm talking about trust. When someone loses your trust it can have far-reaching and devastating results. The chance of you fully trusting that person again is between slim and none. The fact is, you might not trust anyone ever again.

Divorce, rape, abuse, even just a lie—any of these things in a person's life can make them quit trusting. Sometimes you are so bent on never trusting people that you don't know how to get on with life. Here are some ideas to help you start trusting again:

Pray. We have a big God who cares and doesn't want you to be afraid of trusting people. Also, start by trusting a person whom you know, in your mind, is safe. Even if your heart screams "don't trust," give the person a chance. Sometimes our logic has to override our emotions. It'll take time, but you have to start trusting people in order to be effective in the lives of others.

Spend time with the wise and you will become wise, but the friends of fools will suffer. > > > >

## >> Proverbs 13:20

Do you act different around certain people? You are usually shy, but when you get around your friend Chuck your whole personality changes. It feels like he can make you do anything. One time, when you were on the bus with him, he dared you to put your gum into the ear of the guy sitting in front of you. The guy's hair was all messed up and he looked a little rough. Normally, you wouldn't do something so stupid, but something about Chuck made you feel crazy enough to do it. As soon as the gum sticks to his ear, the guy turns around and looks ready to kill you. And you know what? You kind of deserve it.

If you're going to change your personality based on who you hang out with, you'd better carefully pick the people you hang out with. Why don't you pick friends who make you do smart things? How do you act around your friends and what can they make you do?

> But if any of you needs wisdom, you should ask God for it. He is generous and enjoys giving to all people, so he will give you wisdom. >>>>>>>>>>

We all have a lot of things we want, but what do we really need? Most of us have a list a mile long, but when we get right down to it, most of these are wants.

One thing that we all need and can never get enough of is wisdom. Having wisdom will help us to distinguish between what are needs and what are wants. Wisdom gives us the ability to know the difference between right and wrong. It helps us make good decisions. Wisdom that comes from God helps us to know exactly how God wants us to live.

Notice that I'm not talking about being smart. There are a lot of smart people on the earth who aren't very wise. You might know some at your school. They have a high GPA, but they seem to be a few sandwiches short of a picnic. You might wonder how that can be. Well, the thing is, smarts has nothing to do with wisdom. Smart means you have a lot of knowledge, but it doesn't guarantee wisdom. And God never said he would give us intelligence. He said that He would give us wisdom. Why don't you ask for some right now?

All Scripture is given by God and is useful for teaching, for showing people what is wrong in their lives, for correcting faults, and for teaching how to live right. >>>>>>>>>>>>>>>>>>>>>>>

Your parents talk differently to you now than they did when you were a baby. Then you got a lot of "goo-goos" and big smiles, you know—baby talk. But as you grew up, the way your parents treated you changed. When you were a toddler, they probably got tired of all the why questions you asked. In grade school you started to have actual conversations with them. As a teenager, you talked like friends. Throughout your life your parents have talked to you, giving you wisdom and direction.

Do you realize that God has done the same thing? He talks to you differently as you grow in your relationship with Him. Do you remember when you realized He was telling you how much He loved you? What about when you found out how sin damages your relationship? Can you recall the different things God has taught you through His Word? When you read your Bible, underline key passages. Underline the words that are speaking to you about an issue you are working on or dealing with in your life. Note the date—write it down in the margin by the underlined words. It makes a nice record book. You can go back later and see how God was working in your life at certain times.

## >> Hebrews 13:8

Some things change. That's just the way life is. If you don't believe me, check out your school pictures. Start with first grade and go from there. How much have you changed? You might have had freckles, braces, been a different size, had a different haircut, but now it's changed. We often like change, even look forward to it. If the current fads don't suit you, no worries. They'll be different next month. Some changes are good, some are not so good. It's just a matter of perspective.

Some things don't change. Like two plus two. It equals four. It always has. As far as I can tell, it always will. Jesus never changes either. You might hear people say Jesus was "this thing" or Jesus was "that thing," but the truth is simple. Jesus is the same today as He was when He walked the earth two thousand years ago. And that doesn't mean He's out of date. He hasn't changed because He hasn't had to—He's perfect.

If someone tells you something they claim Jesus said, but you can't find it in the Bible, He probably didn't say it. He hasn't changed. Our world has changed, we have changed, our viewpoints have changed. Jesus hasn't changed.

How has your relationship with Jesus changed over the years?

189

## >> Luke 12: 19-21

Then I can say to myself, "I have enough good things stored to last for many years. Rest, eat, drink, and enjoy life!" But God said to him, "Foolish man! Tonight your life will be taken from you. So who will get those things you have prepared for yourself?" This is how it will be for those who store up things for themselves and are not rich toward God. >>>>>>>>>>>>>>>>>>>>>>>>>>>>>

What is your most prized possession? Look around you right now. What holds the most value for you? I happen to own a 1966 Mustang convertible. It is candy apple red and from a distance looks totally hot. When you get up close you can see the torn seats, the missing front bumper, some missing lights. Suddenly it doesn't look so great. It doesn't matter to me. It is one of my most prized possessions. I love it. But not more than my friends, family, or God.

There are things and then there are relationships. Things—cars, skateboards, clothes, jobs, houses—can get damaged. But they can be fixed, sometimes easily, or even replaced. Relationships are a different story. They cannot be easily fixed and never replaced. It takes work to fix a broken relationship. A lot of work.

Even though I have a lot of prized possessions, I will not put those things over my relationships, especially my family and God. Maybe you have a lot of "toys." Do they come before your relationships? How do you know?

You and your friends are just hanging out, having a good time during lunch at school. You're doing the usual guy thing—slamming each other with your talk. In the middle of some of the best slamming you've heard lately, your friend Adrienne comes up to talk with you. You and she have had some good badgering sessions, so in the spirit of the conversation, you slam her in front of everyone. Your friends give you the "ouch" look as she walks away, obviously hurt. You know it was rude, but if she didn't want it to happen she should have stayed away, right? Nope.

Now comes the tough part. You have to ask her for forgiveness. You were wrong, and you need to make it right. And, you've gotta do it in front of the same people you dissed her in front of. You find her after school and apologize. She says it's no big deal, but you know it is. You tell her you want to apologize in front of the guys, and she looks at you like you're crazy. But the next day you do it, and you can tell she really appreciates it. And the guys respect the guts it took too.

When you tease, like many of us like to do, you'd better know when you've taken it too far. It's easy to do and hard to notice. Never make it worse by blowing it off. Make it right.

191

The LORD's voice shakes the oaks and strips the leaves off the trees. In his Temple everyone says, "Glory to God!" >>>>>>>>>>>>>>>>>>>

In 1992, the United States put together the greatest basketball team ever assembled. They were called the Dream Team because no one, up to that point, could imagine that much talent on one team. Every player was great. As they got into the competition at the Olympics, no team they played had a chance. Most of their opponents just looked forward to the team pictures before each game. They really didn't care that much about actually playing. You know why? Because they were in such awe of Team USA. They were that good. Everyone had so much respect for the Dream Team that they basically gave up before the game was ever played!

How in awe of God are you? Say these words, right now, out loud: Water, pour out of the ceiling. Did it happen? Do you realize that when God speaks, it happens? Just His saying the words makes it happen. Maybe we have forgotten how powerful God is!

When you go to church, what are your feelings? Do you respect God or just show up to see people? Do you believe that what He says will happen?

## >> Matthew 20:20-22a

Jesus asked, "What do you want?" Wow! What a question. You don't find it very often in the Bible, God

Then the wife of Zebedee came to Jesus with her sons. She bowed before him and asked him to do something for her. Jesus asked, "What do you want?" She said, "Promise that one of my sons will sit at your right side and the other will sit at your left side in your kingdom." But Jesus said, "You don't understand what you are asking. Can you drink the cup that I am about to drink?" >> >> >

asking you "What do you want?" I know if He were to ask me that question my list would be a mile long. I don't think I would give the politically correct answer: world peace. That is nice, but it wouldn't be the first thing out of my mouth if God were to ask me what I wanted.

What is interesting about this passage is that Jesus addresses what she wants, but He deals with what she needs. Mrs. Zebedee wants her sons to be important, to sit at a place of honor next to Jesus. And how does Jesus respond? He tells her that she doesn't understand what she is asking for, and dives into her real need—her need to know the price that must be paid to sit at His side.

The real need is humility. That is the price to be paid. The kind of humility that doesn't ask the question "How great will I (or my sons) be?" Maybe you want to be important because you don't feel like you are. Maybe God doesn't let you feel that way because He needs you to be humble.

"And when she finds it, she will call her friends and neighbors and say, 'Be happy with me because I have found the coin that I lost.'" >>>>>>>>

How bad do you want your friends to know Jesus? Come on now, answer honestly. Think about it. How much would your life change if your best non-Christian friend became a Christian? I think we sometimes give lip-service to evangelism. We say how much we want to see our friends know Jesus, but in truth we like the fact that they don't. It is easy to go out with our non-Christian friends and dive into some drinking, drugs, or whatever, because they don't have the convictions we do. If they became a Christian then all of that would change.

Often, when those who are far from the kingdom walk into it, we aren't as excited as we should be. How sad! Jesus lets us know that there is a lot of partying in heaven when someone gives their life to God. So why not try it? Throw a party! Help your non-Christian friends get personal relationships with Christ. And then throw a BIG party for them. Try it—heaven's having one.

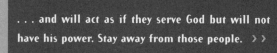

... and will act as if they serve God but will not have his power. Stay away from those people. >>

You might know one of these people. Their spiritual life looks so together. They are committed to ministry. They always say they want to have a godly character. They might even confront you on your lack of godliness. They want people to see them when they pray. They talk about how many tracts they've handed out, and they quote a lot of Bible verses from memory. But there is something wrong. They say what they should say, they look "spiritually good," but there is something wrong. If you look deeper, you notice that they play the part well, but there is no fruit in their life. There isn't anyone who has come to faith in Jesus, or had their faith increased, because of the ministry of this person who looks good. Maybe they have bought into the appearance of a good lifestyle, but that's as deep as it goes. Jesus said in Matthew 7:17 that "every good tree produces good fruit." What fruit is evident in their life? Is it good? Now ask yourself an even harder question: What kind of fruit are you producing? Is it good?

There will be more and more evil in the world, so most people will stop showing their love for each other. >>>>>>>>>>>>>>>>>>>>>>>>>>>>

## >> Matthew 24:12

He is the most annoying person you know. He always has something smart to say and he always has to have the last word. Most of the time you wish you didn't know him at all!

He wants to take a girl out on a date. She told him the only way she'd go is if he got a date for her friend and they went double. He comes to you, because he figures you'll agree to go. You tell him no and you mean it. But he offers to pay for everything and to sweeten the pot, he offers to pay you as well! It is obvious that he won't leave you alone, so you finally agree. During the date you hardly say a word and are basically a butt to everyone. You feel justified because you didn't want to go in the first place. You have a terrible time, but you figure it's okay because you scored some cash on the deal.

Have things gone so bad in your life that you forget what it is to be a friend? Even if a person totally annoys you, can't you be nice? You might be the only person he trusts! He may not have any other friends.

Sometimes we have to put aside our personal feelings and do things for others. Do it just because it is the right thing to do—not for money, not for notoriety—but because it's right and you can.

Also, women should wear proper clothes that show respect and self control, not using braided hair or gold or pearls or expensive clothes. >>>>>>>>

What is modesty? Have you ever wondered how it's defined? What does Paul mean when he tells people to dress modestly? Like, is that nothing above the knee? Only turtlenecks? No skin showing anywhere on your entire body?

Some parents are bothered that girls are wearing tank tops with their bra straps hanging out. They don't like their daughter's belly buttons hanging out for all to see, and they really lose it when they pierce their tongue. For guys it is the baggy pants with underwear showing, always wearing shorts and loving to look like they just woke up.

So we still haven't answered the question. Truth is, the definition changes from culture to culture. What is modest in France may not be modest in the United States. So here are two things to remember:

1. Listen to your parents. They provide for you and you should honor them enough to hear what they have to say. Try to agree on your choice of clothes.

2. Go look in a full-length mirror. Right now. Go. How we dress is an expression of who we are. So ask yourself this: "What am I advertising?" Do you like the answer? Better yet, does God?

197

> Crowds of people were coming and going so that Jesus and his followers did not even have time to eat. He said to them, "Come away by yourselves, and we will go to a lonely place to get some rest." >>

Plan a day next week so you have nowhere to go and nowhere to be. Take off your watch and put away the clocks you normally look at. Slow down for a day. Enjoy it, seeing what life can be like in a world that is not so rushed.

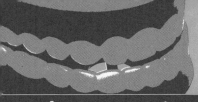

And from far away the LORD appeared to his people and said, "I love you people with a love that will last forever. That is why I have continued showing you kindness." >>>>>>>>>>>>>>>>>>>>>

It's a love story that never gets old. The story of how much God loves us and, because of that love, extends kindness to us. Maybe you have been on a mission trip or to a camp where it was totally clear that God was working. You felt like God was walking by you every moment you were there. You would do anything to keep that feeling alive when you get home. You just want to feel this way forever. Guess what? You can if you have a personal relationship with Jesus.

God's love is great. You can't get away from it. It has always been here and it will always continue. It isn't a fad or some quickie relationship. It is as real as love gets.

Now think for a moment. God wrote a book and gave His son, Jesus, as a gift to show you how much you mean to Him. So turn the tables. How much do you love God? What do you do to show Him? Here are some ideas: Write God a letter about you, tell a friend about Him, volunteer to work in your church, help out a local charity. When you do for others and tell them about Jesus, you are serving God. When you serve God, you show Him how much you love Him.

I was put to death on the cross with Christ, and I do not live anymore—it is Christ who lives in me. I still live in my body, but I live by faith in the Son of God who loved me and gave himself to save me.

>>>>>>>>>>>>>>>>>>>>>>>>>>>>>>

It's the middle of the school year and you can't believe it, you've gained ten pounds. You're seventeen years old and you notice that you are losing your hair—there is a bald spot forming! You start using chemicals to grow the hair back and dieting to take the weight off. It all comes down to a simple fact: You don't like what you look like. You have plenty of great friends, but when you look in the mirror, you don't like the person you see.

If you're not careful, you could sink into a deep depression and, without serious help, have a lot of trouble coming out of it. So how do you begin to accept who you are when you don't like yourself? It's not easy—but you have to start by figuring out who you are to God. If you're a Christian, He lives in you. That should give you some direction! It's what's inside that counts.

Listen, people shouldn't care about your looks. They should care about what's inside and accept you for who you are. If they don't, maybe it is time to find new friends.

## >> Luke 15:29-30

"But the older son said to his father, 'I have served you like a slave for many years and have always obeyed your commands. But you never gave me even a young goat to have at a feast with my friends. But your other son, who wasted all your money on prostitutes, comes home, and you kill the fat calf for him!'" >>>>>>>>>>>>>>>>>>>>>>>>>

Why is it that we go through life loving God, trying to do all the Bible says, sharing our faith, but we just can't seem to catch a break? It's just not fair! All around us are people who don't give a rip about their commitment to Christ, and they seem to have things so good! Even worse, we see non-Christians who have everything going their way. They have the hot dates, the cash, and parents who let them do whatever they want.

You are secure in who you are, you like what God is doing in your life, but you're sick of seeing people catch breaks when they don't deserve it. At least you don't think they deserve it. They get blessed no matter what but you have to work for your blessings.

Quit comparing yourself to others! The only person you have to measure up to is the person God wants you to be: yourself. Are you living up to your full potential? Are you looking more like Jesus? That's what you should be focusing on, not everyone else! Just look at yourself, and love those people you think are catching all the breaks.

## >> 1 Corinthians 8:5-6

Even though there are things called gods, in heaven or on earth (and there are many "gods" and "lords"), for us there is only one God—our Father. All things came from him, and we live for him. And there is only one Lord—Jesus Christ. All things were made through him, and we also were made through him.

>>>>>>>>>>>>>>>>>>>>>>>>>>>>>

From a distance he seems cool, but anybody with that much going for him must be too good to be true. His girlfriend seems nice enough, but you figure both of them are out of your league. His name is in the paper all the time. He likes to race dirt bikes and he usually wins. Then you hear that he told someone he doesn't like the football types 'cause they don't "live on the edge enough." "Forget him," you think.

One day you pass him coming in as you are leaving a convenience store. You exchange grunts (which in cool guy language means "hello"). Your car won't start—the stupid engine won't crank. You let loose some regrettable words and look up to see Mr. Dirt Bike in front of you. He tells you to pop the hood. He tweaks the motor and it starts right up. You thank him and end up hanging out for a couple of hours, talking in the parking lot. Turns out the rumors were wrong. He's a good guy and you have a lot in common. By the time you graduate, he is one of your best friends. All because you took the time to get to know him and accept him.

How is this similar to your relationship with God? Do you really know Him or do you just know some stuff about Him?

> "I am the LORD your God, who holds your right hand, and I tell you, 'Don't be afraid. I will help you.' >>>>>>>>>>>>>>>>>>>>>>>>>>>>>

## >> Isaiah 41:13

There are a lot of opportunities for you to serve God. Don't believe me? The next time you're online type "summer missions" into your search engine and see what happens. So why not get involved? What keeps you from fully experiencing the Christian life by serving others? You don't have to do a mission trip. You could just help out in your youth group, or in another ministry at your church. Are you afraid that they're going to make you work—that you might actually have to do something? If you would rather just sit at home and do nothing, that's your choice, but how does that help God's kingdom?

If you're scared because you might have to leave your comfort zone and do stuff that you might not like, welcome to the real world. At least try it! Set the fear aside and talk to God. He will go before you and help you. That might sound like a cheesy church answer, but it's true. If you ask Him, He'll help you. Is it money? Do you think you can't go on a mission trip because you can't afford it? Go ahead and ask God to provide.

Take a serious look at what keeps you from doing ministry. It might come down to being scared of what you can't do instead of trusting God to help you do what you can. Go ahead. Look up those websites. How can you help?

## >> 1 Peter 2:11-12

Dear friends, you are like foreigners and strangers in this world. I beg you to avoid the evil things your bodies want to do that fight against your soul. People who do not believe are living all around you and might say that you are doing wrong. Live such good lives that they will see the good things you do and will give glory to God on the day when Christ comes again. >>>>>>>>>>>>>>>>>>>

Be who you are—be real. Don't try to be something you're not. Don't present a false image of yourself to fool people! Don't be a hypocrite.

You know the type I'm talking about. At church they have all the answers for every question. They can give out eloquent prayers, using the "thees" and "thous" and even "hark." They look great at church. But they are someone else at school. They have a reputation for being one of the biggest partyers around. You see them stoned at the game on Friday but looking angelic by Sunday morning. You can't believe they can show their face! You decide you are going to confront them—to let them know what they are doing is wrong. You've discussed it with everyone else in the group, and they agree with you. "Go get 'em" they tell you.

Stop right now. Before you do anything, think about the gossip that's been going on in the group. Yeah, right, it's not like getting stoned—or is it? Sin is sin. Instead of confronting the party animal, try this: Pray for them, and deal with your own personal issues first.

If someone is lazy, the roof will begin to fall. If he doesn't fix it, the house will leak. ＞＞＞＞＞＞＞＞＞

## ＞＞ Ecclesiastes 10:18

I don't feel like writing today. I have better things to do, like watch TV. This book wouldn't be very long if I got lazy and didn't finish. In fact, this book wouldn't exist. Simple idea: Each day do at least one productive activity. Instead of resting for six days and working for one, do the opposite. Don't ever give people the opportunity to accuse you of being lazy.

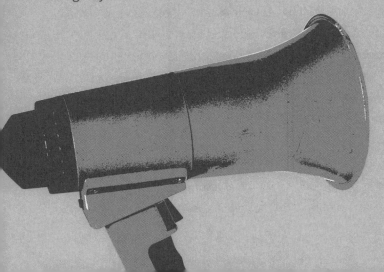

## >> Psalm 100

Shout to the LORD, all the earth. Serve the Lord with joy; come before him with singing. Know that the LORD is God. He made us, and we belong to him; we are his people, the sheep he tends. Come into his city with songs of thanksgiving and into his courtyards with songs of praise. Thank him and praise his name. The LORD is good. His love is forever, and his loyalty goes on and on. >>>>>

Have you ever been around someone who's always negative? No matter what the situation, in their opinion there is always something wrong. Come on, you know the type. They might have a hundred things going great in their life, but they will focus on the one downer, no matter how small it is!

Take Amber. She was getting straight A's at school, made the local youth symphony playing her french horn, and her boyfriend was the nicest guy at school. But she was really upset because Karen, her boyfriend's ex, sat two rows behind her in English and whispered something to the girl next to her. She was just sure Karen was talking about her. It ruined her whole day.

Do you know Amber? Maybe you are Amber! You can't think of anything to be positive about. If that's the case, read the last verse of Psalm 100. God is good! Look for all the awesome things of God in your life. And teach other people to do the same! Look for ways to be positive.

> I am guiding you in the way of wisdom, and I am leading you on the right path. ❯ ❯ ❯ ❯ ❯ ❯ ❯ ❯ ❯ ❯

## ❯❯ Proverbs 4:11

You think your Mom is so old-fashioned. Who in the world, at least your world, has to be in by midnight on the weekends? You are in your prime—old enough to have some independence, and now she has to dream up this stupid rule! You live by it for a while. Then comes the weekend your friends are going out to a bonfire. It's a drive out to this place. You know you want to stay out past midnight, but why ask. Your mom will just say no—she always does. So you don't get permission, you just break the rule. When you stroll in at 2:45 A.M., your mom is furious. She had no idea where you were and was very worried. She watched some show on drunk driving, and it really freaked her out. You're toast. She takes your keys and grounds you for a month from the phone, the Internet, and weekends out!

Face it, you pushed the envelope, now you have to pay the consequences. Next time you want to change the rules, you should try asking for permission first. Be wise! Even if you think there is no way—ask first, and negotiate something that is acceptable to your parents. There is a big difference between independence and rebellion. Choose the right path.

## >> James 3:16

Do you know people who have to have everything their way? It's all
one-sided. Picture this: You are goofing off and squirt a friend with
some water. He gets mad about it and refuses to talk to you for a week.
Then one day, he dumps a bucket of water on your head. You are
irritated—but he tells you "lighten up. It's only water!" With this person
you can only do what he wants on the weekends, only listen to his
music in the car, and only play the video games he wants to play or he
doesn't want to hang with you.

Do you have friendships that are this one-sided? Which person are
you—the one who only wants it his way? Do you think life is just about
you? Why don't you put a broken mirror in your room or your locker to
remind you of this important fact: Life is not just about you. And maybe
you need to tell a friend or two about the broken mirror.

You and your brother are hanging out one night. He asks you if you want to go outside and do something cool. Of course you do. When you get outside, he's got a firecracker. It's different—it's encased in metal. It looks like a mini-bomb with a short fuse. You ask him what he wants to do, and he says, "Light it!" You look at the really short fuse and hesitate. He tells you it will be fine. He should know, he's the "older" brother. And so, even though you're not sure you should, you light it. Your brother starts to throw it, but it blows up in his hand! It makes a huge noise, and you both take off, running into the house.

His hand is bleeding bad, but you don't want to tell your parents. He goes through the night in pain, and when the morning comes you have no choice but to 'fess up. At the hospital, the doctors take the metal out of your brother's hand and lecture you both on what a dumb thing you did.

Don't deny the foolish things you do, own up to them. Better yet, avoid doing them in the first place! They can have huge consequences that go beyond yourself. If you're not sure about something you're about to do, think it through! Thinking about it before you act will pay off.

When pride comes, then comes shame. ⟩⟩⟩⟩⟩

## ⟩⟩ Proverbs 11:2a

You're hanging out with all your friends on Saturday night. You're playing video games, listening to music, and eating nachos. About 11:00, Michelle shows up with a couple of her friends. It's cool. You're having a good time. Suddenly Michelle says she thinks the party needs a little more life, and she breaks out some alcohol. Now all of a sudden the atmosphere has changed. "It's okay. Drinking is okay; getting drunk is what's wrong," she says. Everyone agrees, and the drinks start pouring. What do you do? If you drink, you're agreeing with it. You know it's not right because you are under 21. If you don't drink they will say you're a loser.

You know what to do. Get away before trouble starts. You should always have a plan. Have a plan. What is it?

It is not good to eat too much honey, nor does it bring you honor to brag about yourself. >>>>>

Elizabeth is always bragging about what she has accomplished. When she was picked to paint the mural in the school commons, you could hardly stand to be around her. She is always quick to tell you how much she has done, and even quicker to ask you if you've noticed. She loves to talk about all the guys that are asking her out, and how all their dads think she is hot too. Man, your gag reflex is working overtime, 'cause she makes you want to puke.

How can someone who seems so nice be so stuck on herself? There are a lot of possible answers, but it's probably coming from a poor self-image. People like Elizabeth are usually busy putting themselves on a pedestal because they figure that if they don't do it, no one will. They might have a crappy family situation, and the only way they can feel important is by bragging—whether it's real stuff or just made up.

If you have a good friend like Elizabeth, talk to him or her about it. Let them know that you like them for who they are, not what they've done. And let them know that God loves them too!

**"You will search for me. And when you search for me with all your heart, you will find me!"** >>>

## >> Jeremiah 29:13

Is God real? It's a common question. Some say no, that there is no proof of the existence of God, so there is no God. They think everything can be explained by science, never considering a universal God. Then there are those who believe there are many gods or that God is simply whatever you want God to be. Maybe God is a tree, or a golf club, or even a light bulb—if it works for you, then it is right.

Do you ever get confused when you hear these arguments? Do they start to make some sense to you and make you doubt your faith? Do you think they can't be right, but wonder if you're wrong? Answer this: Have you ever seen God work? If you say yes then how do you know it was God and not just fate? Hmmm . . .

There is only one real God. And if you want to be sure of that, you have to search for Him. He will become more real to you as you learn more about Him and surrender yourself to Him. You have to take the time to learn about Him (in other words, read your Bible). Take the time to communicate with Him (also known as prayer). And you have to quit just looking at yourself (meaning you must focus on others). He is real and there is only one God. Make Him more real in your life.

>>> >>> >>>

Be humble under God's powerful hand so he will lift you up when the right time comes. Give all your worries to him, because he cares about you. >>>

>> i Peter 5:6-7

"Nobody likes me, everybody hates me, guess I'll go eat worms . . ." You've heard the song before. When you go to church, you hear that God cares and you need to tell Him what is going on in your life. But sometimes that just doesn't cut it. You really want to tell Him, but without a physical person there, it feels sort of empty—like you're not really giving the worries away to anyone.

Maybe all you need is to be able to visualize it. Take an empty can and remove any label on it. Then put your own label on it—one that says "worries." Keep the can on a shelf. Every time you get uptight about something, go to the shelf and pray, asking God to take your worries and hold them from you. Leave them in the can with God. You may find that you need more than one can.

He gave himself for us so he might pay the price to free us from all evil and to make us pure people who belong only to him—people who are always wanting to do good deeds. >>>>>>>>>>>>

Did you ever see the movie *City Of Angels*? The main character is an angel (played by Nicholas Cage) who falls in love with a woman (Meg Ryan) and gives up being an angel to be with her. I'm not going to debate the theology. I'm going to ask a question. There is a scene toward the end of the movie, after Meg Ryan's character dies, when Nicholas Cage's character is sitting alone and crying. Here he is, having given up his angel status to become a man, and now the woman he loves has been killed in an accident. Another angel comes to offer comfort, and Cage asks him the tough question: "Is God punishing me?" The angel responds, "You know better than that." This, I think, is a great answer.

God doesn't punish us for sin. Sin has it's own consequences. If God punished us for all our sins, then we would be paying the price. If we have to pay the price, why did Jesus die on the cross in our place?

Don't believe God is punishing you. Sometimes things—bad things—happen. Those are the consequences of our sinful world. Learn all you can from the bad experiences. And don't blame God for them, let Him help you through them.

> **Always be joyful. Pray continually, and give thanks whatever happens. That is what God wants for you in Christ Jesus.** > > > > > > > >

>> **1 Thessalonians 5:16-18**

Have you ever wondered what God wants for you and your life? Sometimes we call it "finding God's will." That's just a way of saying that we are trying to find out what God wants us to do with our life.

Which is easier: your parents telling you to take out the trash every Tuesday, or just letting it pile up and hoping you'll figure out that you should dump it? Well, obviously it's easier if they tell you to dump the trash on Tuesday. If they just let it go, you may figure it out, but maybe you won't!

I've got some good news for you. It is actually very easy to figure out what God's will for your life is. He tells us what he wants us to do in the Bible. Many passages are very specific. This is one of them. He wants you to have a great attitude (always joyful). He wants you to talk to Him—God—about everything (pray continually). And He wants you to be grateful for all that you receive (give thanks). If you follow this, you will be living out the "will of God."

Sometimes we try to make it way too hard for ourselves! Like it's some big mystery. It isn't. It's clearly written in the Word. He wants us to get it! Now that you know some of God's will for your life, how are you living it out?

Those who want to do right more than anything else are happy, because God will fully satisfy them.

>>>>>>>>>>>>>>>>>>>>>>>>>>>>>>>>

Does God really make a difference in our life? Think about it for a minute. Okay, time's up.

There are a lot of really good people in the world who don't claim to be Christians. There are also a lot of people out there who do claim to be Christians. They might wear all the T-shirts and other Christian paraphernalia—and yet they seem to not be very nice. So if people can be good without God and others can be bad with God, we come back to the question. Does God really make a difference?

The issue here is in our motivation behind what we do. We need to love God and people so that He can make a difference in the world around us. As we serve others for God, we start to understand His plan. He wants to meet needs, and He uses us as His tools to mend hurting people. We can't deny that there are "bad" people who are Christians, but we must let God deal with them. For all those people out there who aren't Christians but have big hearts, let's show them how to have a real purpose behind their acts of kindness. Help them see how God can fully satisfy them.

"Now, therefore, make confession to the Lord God of your fathers, and do His will: separate yourselves from the peoples of the land, and from pagan wives." >>>>>>>>>>>>>>>>>>>>>>>>>>>>>>

>> Ezra 10:11

Do you collect stuff? If you're a girl, maybe you have been collecting bracelets for the last ten years. You have collected hundreds and once in a while you like to just sit down and look at them. There is one that stands out. You keep it in a special place, separate from the rest. It is pure gold with a diamond, and you inherited it from your great-grandmother.

Maybe you're a guy and you've collected sports cards. You have thousands. You love to look through them occasionally. Most are in boxes, but the special ones are in notebooks. Then you have those three Michael Jordan rookie cards—those are locked away because of their value.

Set apart. That's what God wants for our lives. That is what He is talking about when he says to be holy—it means set apart.
If you're a Christian, you're not like everybody else. You are different for a reason. So set yourself apart for God. Be different, and when people notice it tell them why. You are setting yourself apart, being holy.

You are the salt of the earth. But if the salt loses its salty taste, it cannot be made salty again. It is good for nothing, except to be thrown out and walked on. >>>>>>>>>>>>>>>>>>>>>>>>>

What kind of "taste" do you leave behind with people who have been around you? Is it bitter, something they gag on? That might be the case if you try to throw out too much of your opinion without doing any listening. People might accept you to your face, but they can't wait for you to leave. Like too much salt, they can't wait to spit you out. Remember, a little bit of salt used the right way enhances the flavor of the things it contacts. Think about popcorn. With no salt, it is okay. With too much salt, you probably won't eat it. But with the right amount of salt the popcorn is awesome.

Jesus used salt as an illustration to help us understand how we need to live our lives. We need to make the incredible difference by giving the right amount. If we pour out too much, we make people sick—we turn them off. Put an empty salt shaker on top of your computer or on your desk. Do you make things better or worse?

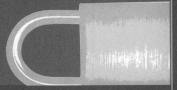

## ❯❯ Ecclesiastes 10:3

One day you see Jakob walking down the hall, and it looks like he is crying or at least has been crying. He is obviously very upset. "Jakob, what's up?" you call out, wanting to show your concern.

He looks at you and starts telling you how tired he is of being picked on in his science class. It's not just the other guys, the teacher joins in. He just tries to mind his own business, but they won't stop. Then he tells you that he's had it and tomorrow he's going to settle some things. You ask him what he means by that. "I'll bring the fire power to create my own justice," he replies. "You're crazy!" you respond. "Jakob, you're not really going to do anything stupid, are you?" Jakob says, "We'll see," and takes off. You figure he is just angry and shooting off his mouth. He'll get over it. You do nothing—just let it go.

The next day school gets out early because someone else was wise enough to tell an authority about Jakob's threats. He was caught with two guns at school. Fortunately no one was hurt. You could have done something, but didn't. Now who is the fool?

> How terrible it will be for people who think they are wise and believe they are clever. >>>>>>>

You know everything, and you know it. No? Then maybe it's someone you know. They believe they know it all. They talk down to people all the time. You have watched them laugh at someone who messes up a word when reading out loud. They have just one friend—one who is just like them—and together they have a bad habit of putting people down and rejecting them.

When Isaiah wrote this passage, he put these people into perspective. He says it is terrible for them. Have you ever wondered why these people don't get what they deserve? Well, in a way they do. They have to live with themselves. They don't usually have a lot of friends. And they spend a lot of energy proving that they know more than anyone. The truth is, there is always someone who knows more. It's terrible for them because they are living a lie. A lie they desperately want others to believe.

Help them. Let them know that you know what you are talking about and move on.

## >> James 1:26

Straight up five on five, a time of basketball with the guys that you have looked forward to since it was planned last week. When you get there, you see Paul has shown up. Paul is an okay guy, until he steps on the basketball court. Then he develops a major attitude. As soon as you get in the game his mouth just starts going. You can stand the trash talk, but he's got nothing to back it up. He can't play. He can barely dribble, can't shoot, and anyone can score on him. But he's always telling everyone to get with it, that they've got no game, and that he'll school you if you try to guard him. You want to guard him, so you can show him up. You always work him over good.

Think about your spiritual life. Are you all talk, or can you play the game? If you can play the game, are you in the game? Every time you watch basketball, think about your spiritual life and how you play in God's game.

## >> Titus 3:1

Teachers. One simple word that brings a ton of different thoughts. There are some you love, some you hate, some you agree with, and others who have ideas that make you wonder where they are coming from.

You and your friends agree, for the most part, about who is a good teacher and who isn't. But you have one big problem with the teachers you can't stand. You are a smart mouth to them. Take Mr. Perkins' class. You know he doesn't like you any more than you like him. So what do you do? You sit front and center in the classroom. It drives him crazy. When he calls on you, you make sure your answer is only half true so it will throw him off. You get others talking while he is trying to teach. You disrupt at key moments. And the worst part is, you like being this way. Mr. Perkins wants to kick you out. But it's a required class and his is the only one that fits your schedule.

It might be fun, but it's wrong. Let's not even mention what a bad witness it is to act this way. Let's just note that your teachers need your help and your respect, not your ridicule. How can you help and not hurt?

You're sitting in a coffee shop across the street from school. At a table near yours, you watch some teasing going on between a guy and a girl. They are obviously good friends. You notice the guy is really into his verbal punches, laughing after every slam. She isn't laughing much. She looks like she is trying to give him the message to stop. As the conversation continues, it becomes obvious that she doesn't like what is being said. Obvious, that is, to everyone but the guy doing all the talking! She should be able to just tell him to stop, but for some reason she doesn't. Finally he pushes the teasing over the edge. You watch as she stands up and screams "to hell with you!" and walks out.

The guy just sits there laughing, thinking she is kidding. But as she takes off down the street, he is suddenly stunned. He doesn't know what to do or say. Should he go after her, let her calm down, or just let it go? Well, I don't know. He never should have let it get that far. He should have picked his words more carefully and been in tune with the nonverbal vibes he was getting!

Before you tease, make sure you know them well enough to know when to stop. It might save a friendship.

223

So Jacob worked for Laban seven years so he could marry Rachel. But they seemed like just a few days to him because he loved Rachel very much. >>>

Barry and Camille have been going together for five weeks. From Barry's perspective, everything is going great. They like each other, don't fight, and have fun together. At this point, Camille decides to let Barry look at some of her journal. He reads a bunch of stuff that she has written about him. Stuff like how much she is falling in love with Barry. He is a little freaked about the word *love*. He really likes Camille, but love? That is a whole different story, one he's not sure about. When he asks her about what she wrote, Camille tells him that she sees them spending the rest of their lives together. "Whoa! What about college?" he asks. She explains to him that she plans on moving wherever he goes. She can wait to go to school. She'll just get a job. That way they can be together. Now Barry is really freaked and confused. How can a girl he has only dated for five weeks be ready for marriage? Why would she throw her own education away for him? Does he even love her?

Marriage is a huge commitment. One that cannot be taken lightly. Look at Jacob! If a relationship is meant to be, it will work out. But don't ever push the issue. It is much better to wait and be right than to rush and be wrong!

## >> Deuteronomy 6:10-12

Success is always good, right? Andrea thought so. She applied herself wholeheartedly to everything she committed to.

> The LORD your God will bring you into the land he promised to your ancestors, to Abraham, Isaac, and Jacob, and he will give it to you. The land has large, growing cities you did not build, houses full of good things you did not buy, wells you did not dig, and vineyards and olive trees you did not plant. You will eat as much as you want. But be careful! Do not forget the Lord, who brought you out of the land of Egypt where you were slaves. >>>>>>>>>>>

She studied ballet, practicing five days a week and giving four recitals a year. On the yearbook staff she became the editor. It consumed her time—she put in many hours every week. In the end, her high school yearbook won some national awards. She was also a state qualifier on the debate team. It might not sound like the most exciting life to you, but she was successful, earning scholarships and praise. In fact, she was so successful that she forgot about her church and devotion to God.

It has been said that if Satan can't make you sin, he'll make you busy. Andrea was successful at good things but forgot the one thing that could make *her* good.

We all make many mistakes. If people never said anything wrong, they would be perfect and able to control their entire selves, too. >>>>>>>>>>

It isn't enough for you to be good or even great. Your dad wants you to be the best. He lets you know how much he has invested in you: the skis, the lessons, the gas to and from, the days off of work to be at your tournaments. You usually do well, placing almost every time. But the pressure to perform is building. You have to be the best. Anything less will be a failure in your father's eyes.

You take first place at the district meet, and now it's on to the state ski tournament. You do your very best, even managing a personal record. You made a few technical mistakes, but you feel pretty good about your overall effort. In the end, it's only good enough for fourth place. You see your dad working his way through the crowd. He doesn't look happy. He raises his voice, in front of everyone, expressing his disappointment at the results. He accuses you of not really trying. You walk away and get in the car. It's a quiet ride home.

You did your best, and you have that fourth place medal to show for it. You may not be perfect, but no one is—except Jesus.

> But Peter said to Jesus, "Lord, I am ready to go with you to prison and even to die with you!" But Jesus said, "Peter, before the rooster crows this day, you will say three times that you don't know me." >>

We all face pressures. Sometimes pressure pushes us to succeed, sometimes it tears us down into failure.

One of the pressures that tears at many students in ministry today is the pressure to commit to everything. Pressure from the youth pastor, ski trips, small groups, outreach events, leadership training, worship team, drama team, and the list goes on and on. You like to be involved, but it is impossible to commit to everything all year long. You do have other responsibilities outside of church! But when you don't show up for an event, you know the guilt trip is coming. It isn't that you disagree with the ministry. It isn't that you don't like the youth pastor. You simply can't do everything. You already quit the soccer team to have time for church, but you can't quit everything else.

We all have to give a little. You should only commit to what you can handle. It's true that you can't do everything. Don't overdo it! Learn to say no. Discuss it with your parents. Let them know how you feel so they can help you to prioritize.

Peter tried to commit himself to too much. Even after Jesus told him he would blow it, he still couldn't keep his commitments! Do you feel you have to be committed to everything? Are you? How could you do better?

Have you ever had the feeling you can't go on? Life is just too hard? What do you do when the demands are too high and your time is too short? Pull an all-nighter? Stock up on Jolt? Go nuts? Sometimes it seems like it's all you can do just to keep from losing it.

Survivors from shipwrecks have one chance for survival if they are minus a boat. They have to float. People who tread water, trying to stay in control, just waste energy. But if they will relax and float, they can conserve energy. Of course they can't see what's going on, or hear anything but underwater sounds. Totally helpless. At the mercy of every wave.

Next time life gets stressful and the waters start to get too deep—float. Stop treading water. Fight the urge you have to start bailing yourself out, because you don't have enough energy. So just float. Get off alone and surrender yourself to God. Don't freak. Don't plot or scheme or figure anything out, just float. Jesus had a world to save, disciples to lead, millions to heal, lessons to teach, but he loved to float. He knew that there was too much for his human body to handle. So each day he would just float.

"The father said to him, 'Son, you are always with me, and all that I have is yours.'" >>>>>>>>>

I have this black cat who recently moved in. She's an ugly stray. Skinny. Grungy. And has to be with me 24/7. She rubs all over me like she can't get enough love. She freaks when I put her out. But the weird thing is that she cries even when I'm there. When we are outside she walks over to the door and starts cryin', trying to get in. And there I am right behind her saying, "Here I am stupid, just turn around."

It freaked me out the other day when I realized I'm like that cat. I totally love being with God, rubbin' up on His leg, sitting on His lap, but half the time I can't find Him. I'm all, "Where are you? How come you aren't here when I need you?" Stupid thing is, He is! If I would just turn around and get a clue I'd see Him right there. But like that stupid cat, I'm whining for something that is right in front of me if I'd just turn around . . .

"This is how it will be for those who store up things for themselves and are not rich toward God." >>

What are your top three favorite things in the world? List them now. Don't read on until you've done it. Did you say friends, success, music, sports, God? Your answer will tell you, and anyone who is listening, all about where your heart is. Where do you spend most of your time, energy, money? A lot of times we go through life thinkin' we've got this whole God thing under control. You know who He is and you totally respect that, but all of your time goes into other stuff. Who are you trying to kid? God? Good luck!

Fact: anything you can't give up for God is an idol. That's right, an idol, idolatry, idol-rama, idol-fest. If you've got anything that you can't put on the altar and offer up, God ain't the Lord of your life anymore. God wants anything that is between you and Him. He demands your full attention. Whatcha gonna do? Obey? What's He asking you to give up right this minute? Can you do it? Lay it on the altar and burn it up? You might never get it back, *but* you also might get it back bigger and better than before, just like Abraham and Isaac.

**Wash yourselves and make yourselves clean. Stop doing the evil things I see you do. Stop doing wrong.**
> > > > > > > > > > > > > > > > > > > > > > > > > > > >

## >> Isaiah 1:16

You and your friends have tickets to the P.O.D. concert in a city sixty miles away. You are stoked. This is going to be a great night. As you head down the road, you are listening to the band's CD, warming yourselves up for the event. You know all the words and you're all singing along.

Up ahead you see a white Honda swerving through traffic. At first you think they are some kind of jerk driving crazy, but then you realize they are in trouble. The Honda hits the center divider and streaks back across three lanes, landing in the ditch on the right side of the road. A woman jumps out of the car, frantic, looking at the damage. Now you have a dilemma. Do you stop and help or do you keep going?

You don't want to be late for the big concert, so you keep going. You don't know them. Some adult will stop who can actually help. What could you have done anyway? Well, let's see. You could have made sure she and her passengers were all okay. You could have offered to drive her to a phone, or let her use your cell phone, or actually called for help on her behalf. You could have done a lot of things to bring some calm to the situation.

You don't get a lot of opportunities to be a "Good Samaritan," so take them when they come along! It's the right thing to do. If it was you, panicked on the side of the road, you would appreciate the help.

231

> "But seek God's kingdom, and all the other things you need will be given to you." >>>>>>>>>

## >> Luke 12:31

Have you ever played a rousing game of hide and seek? It's late at night. You're out with your friends. There is a bit of fog in the air and everyone runs off to hide, leaving you alone. Your pulse races. You have no idea what's around the corner. Will it be your friends? You are obsessed with finding them. You check behind every dumpster and crawl behind every bush. You have to find them. You must succeed.

Do you feel the same way about God? Wouldn't that be great? You can. There is so much more at stake in finding God than in winning hide and seek, but sometimes it can seem so boring. Have you lost the thrill of the chase? God isn't only in church or only in the Bible. He's all over the place. Just like hide and seek, God can be found anywhere, behind a tree, in the face of a homeless man, in a freak event. God is there to be found, but you have to seek Him. Don't let anything happen without asking where God is in it. You might be surprised what you find.

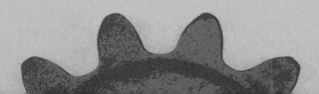

Jesus said, "I tell you the truth, all those who have left houses, brothers, sisters, mother, father, children, or farms for me and for the Good News will get more than they left. Here in this world they will have a hundred times more homes, brothers, sisters, mothers, children, and fields. And with those things, they will also suffer for their belief. But in the age that is coming they will have life forever. >>>>>>>>>>>>>>>>>>>>>>>>>>>>

It is two of the hottest weeks of her life. Not fun hot, heat hot. Liz is on a mission trip to Jamaica, and the temperature is soaring above 90° every day, with lots of humidity. She spends the first week painting everything she comes in contact with. Liz hates to paint. But the buildings need to be painted, so she is willing to do it. At the beginning of the second week, Liz is put on a demolition crew. The crew of six is going to tear apart a ceiling in an office building. It's hot, stuffy, dirty, and Liz loves it. About half way into the job, the crew leader comes in and says he needs two people to leave the demolition crew and go paint. The leader makes the six crew members draw straws. The two short straws have to move on to "paint paradise." Sweet—Liz pulls a long straw.

Jacob pulls a short one but has a great attitude. The thing is, he really likes this demolition stuff and he's good at it. So she offers to trade straws with him.

What are you willing to give up for others? For God? Would you do what's best, even if the other option wasn't necessarily "bad"?

> Anyone who is sick should call the church's elders. They should pray for and pour oil on the person in the name of the Lord. >>>>>>>>>>>>>>>>>

## >> James 5:14

You heard that Tara is sick. She is losing weight and tired all the time. You do the standard "tell her I hope she's feeling better" when you see her mom, but other than that you don't know what to do. You've prayed for her because it sounds like it might be serious. She has been in and out of the hospital, and they are still not sure what is wrong. They just keep doing more tests. You are reading in your Bible and see in Mark 6:13 that the disciples actually anointed people with oil to help in the process of healing. At first you think it sounds weird, but hey—it might help. You call a local Catholic parish and find out how to obtain the oil. Then you get a group of friends together and go to Tara's house one night. You all put your hands on her and pray for God to heal her. As you pray, you pour a little of the oil from the vile onto her forehead. It brings comfort to everyone who takes part, including Tara.

Anointing is a way of showing God that a person is set apart and that you want Him to take notice and heal them. Try it on a sick friend and watch how God works.

234

>> Luke 22:24, 27

The apostles also began to argue about which one of them was the most important. [Jesus replied.] "Who is more important: the one sitting at the table or the one serving? You think the one at the table is more important, but I am like a servant among you." >>>>>>>>>>>>>>>>>>>>>>>>

Ten confessions from an overambitious person:

- I like to get things done, NOW.
- When people get in my way, I will run over them to get what I want.
- I almost always get what I want.
- When I don't get what I want, I will figure out a way to.
- I must feel important.
- I care little for the feelings of others.
- When people confront me, I make the issues theirs—not mine.
- I manipulate all situations I can to work it my way.
- I never admit defeat.
- If at first I don't succeed, I pound it out until I do, even if I'm wrong.

It's not wrong to be ambitious. It's wrong to be overambitious. When we are willing to walk all over people to get something we want badly enough, we are working on our own plan, not God's. What is God's plan for your life? (A biggie.) How does that fit with your ambitions?

We set our eyes not on what we see but on what we cannot see. What we see will last only a short time, but what we cannot see will last forever. >>>>

>> 2 Corinthians 4:18

It is often said that we may never see the results of our ministry efforts until we get to heaven. We will impact people who we come in contact with and not even know it. We may never talk to them, but something we do or the way we treat someone else will make a lasting impression. Many times we are uptight about getting credit for the work we do. We want people to notice the fourteen toilets we cleaned so that the camp bathroom was sanitary. We want people to know that we were the ones who left the party to go get more drinks and snacks for everyone.

It's important to know how we look and what we are looking at when doing these tasks. Look beyond the job. Look at the people it will affect. Don't look at yourself, look at how God can use you if you let Him. Clean toilets won't even last a day, the food will be gone tomorrow. But the impact of these efforts could last a lifetime. Look beyond what you see.

Don't leave your job just because your boss is angry with you. Remaining calm solves great problems.

>>>>>>>>>>>>>>>>>>>>>>>>>>>>>>

John has worked at various jobs over the last three years. Everything from waiting tables to construction work during the summer. He's pretty easygoing, so he figures he can handle working with just about anyone. One summer John's dad decides that John should work for his electric company. John has done odd jobs for his dad before, so this should be an easy way to earn some good money.

Everything is fine until John screws up one of the jobs. He wires a light switch wrong and it fries the breaker. His dad isn't happy. The breaker will have to be replaced. He tells John that he should know better—that he shouldn't be costing him money. John is ticked and tells his dad he is sick of working for him. "You know where the door is," his dad replies. John storms out of there—leaving all his stuff for his dad to pick up. John figures that his leaving will make a dent in his dad's business. What it really causes is a big dent in their relationship.

It is easy to react rashly to situations we don't like, but we shouldn't. We should slow down and respond in a way that will find a solution, not create a bigger problem.

>> Romans 2:1

If you think you can judge others, you are wrong. When you judge them, you are really judging yourself guilty, because you do the same things they do. >>>>>>>>>>>>>>>>>>>>>>>>

What do you do when you go out to eat and you see Dave, one of the leaders of your church, having a beer with dinner? You can't believe it. He and his wife are blatantly sinning right there for everyone to see! You let it go because you don't know exactly what to think about it. One thing is sure, you don't respect him quite as much as you used to.

On New Year's Eve you get invited to a party at your friend's house. This friend just happens to be Dave's son. At 11:45 P.M., Dave breaks out a bottle of champagne to toast in the new year. He also breaks out some sparkling cider. He serves a small amount of champagne to those over twenty-one and cider to everyone else. The clock strikes twelve, everyone drinks their sip of champagne or cider and the party continues.

You are very upset. This time Dave has invited others to sin with him! You have a good mind to tell him what you think. Then you read Romans 2:1.

It is not your job to judge. It's God's. There are sin issues and there are issues of personal preference. Don't confuse the two. They are not the same.

If people please God, God will give them wisdom, knowledge, and joy. But sinners will get only the work of gathering and storing wealth that they will have to give to the ones who please God. So all their work is useless, like chasing the wind. >>>>>>>

There is a saying most of us have grown up with that helps us to understand the benefits of giving. It's found in Acts 20:35, where Jesus says "It is more blessed to give than to receive." It is awesome to give yourself away, your salvation and your stuff. But that doesn't mean it's bad to receive.

I've watched lots of people involved in ministry get burned out because they never know how to receive. They are great givers, no doubt. But like a car, you can only go so far on one tank of gas. Sooner or later you have to receive more fuel for the car to give more effort. We are a lot like a car sometimes. We try to push our miles per gallon to the limit. We fail to get regular fill ups, because it's admitting that we need help!

Learn to receive graciously and regularly. Learn how to let God fill you so that you can continue to give. When you pray, open your hands up like you are receiving a gift. Tell God that you want to receive all that He is willing to give you!

They loved praise from people more than praise from God. > > > > > > > > > > > > > > > > > > > > > > > >

A.J. was a quiet and shy kid all through junior high. When he got to high school, he decided that he wanted to be popular. He had always felt like an outcast—like someone standing on the outside looking in. So A.J. got to be friends with Mike, a popular guy in his English class. He figured Mike could be the in he was looking for. One day, Mike invited A.J. to a party on the coming Friday night. Of course, A.J. went. He sat against the wall, scared to death, not knowing what to do. Then Mike came up and offered A.J. a beer. He drank it, and then had four more. Suddenly A.J. was the life of the party! He would do anything to get attention, and it was working! People were noticing him! It didn't take long for A.J. to reach his goal. He was one of the most popular people in school, famous for his party exploits. Lost in all of this was his commitment to God.

God is able to wait for A.J. to move through this stage of his life—to realize it isn't the way to go. But He shouldn't have to wait. God is the only one we should want to be popular with. He is the only one who counts in the big picture—for all of eternity.

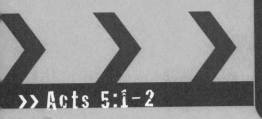

But a man named Ananias and his wife Sapphira sold some land. He kept back part of the money for himself; his wife knew about this and agreed to it. But he brought the rest of the money and gave it to the apostles. > > > > > > > > > > > > > > > > > > >

One was never enough for Mark. He had two nice four-wheel-drive trucks, a boat, a nice mountain bike, and a great pool at his house. But he was never satisfied. He always wanted more. He still wanted jet skis, snow boards, and better hiking equipment. He judged everyone by how much stuff they had, and if it didn't match his pile, he totally dissed them. And if the stuff wasn't brand name, it was junk, and he wouldn't even hang out with them. Mark was so obsessed with what he had and what he wanted that he lost his focus on what he lacked and needed.

Mark was missing the point. He was losing friends because they couldn't keep up with him and couldn't stand him or his lifestyle. After all, not everyone inherits a fat trust fund to buy whatever they want.

Mark has a lot of nice things, but you know what? One day it will all burn. None of that stuff—those toys—will make it to heaven. Mark's friends are another story. They could make it to heaven—if someone would take the time to show them the way. The only things that will last are souls and God's word. So what will you be taking with you to heaven? Think about that one.

241

Your power comes from your ability to know more than everyone else. The more info you have, the more you can hold over people's heads. Anything is fair game. All gossip goes through you and you can't stand not being in the loop of all that is going on. Your pride swells when someone comes up to you and asks, "Have you heard?" and you already know.

Information is power. That's what they say. Whoever "knows," controls. Think about it. It's true. The few people who know the secret formula for Coke have a lot of power. Power to keep the secret. At the same time, it sure can be lonely keeping a secret. It can be very tough knowing everything, always feeling like you can't say much, or you will be gossiping.

Sometimes it's just better not to have all the information, because then you don't have the responsibility that comes with knowing. Before you blurt out the words "tell me," think about what you are going to do with the information. Do you really need to know? Do you really want to know?

>> Luke 2:14

This verse is part of the Christmas story. Remember what it was like waiting for Christmas when you were little? You had no patience, trying your best to wait for the day to arrive. You had to get pictures taken in goofy red and green outfits. Then you had to get more pictures taken while sitting on Santa's lap at the mall. Your parents' favorite line was "you'd better be good or Santa won't bring you anything this year." As you get older and discover the truth about Santa, this doesn't work quite as well for the folks. And the holiday gets a little traditional and even sappy. But I bet you still like watching favorite Christmas movies and eating all the good food and candy.

The angels arrived on that first Christmas with a different battle cry. They told the shepherds to seek peace and please God. This is something we think about more at Christmas, but this is a message for all year 'round. Think about it now. Does your life have peace? Does it encourage peace with others? Does it please God?

## >> Psalm 51:1-2

How many times have you stuck your foot in your mouth? Brenda has done it so many times that if it were an Olympic event, she'd win the gold medal. One day in class, when they were supposed to be discussing *Hamlet*, Brenda and her friends were talking. When one of the girls mentioned an award the school was about to get, Brenda couldn't contain herself. "What a scam!" she said. "How can we win such a prestigious award? We obviously don't have a good Sex Ed program! Look at all the pregnant girls walking around our halls!" She failed to notice Carmen, visibly pregnant, sitting behind her. Brenda was friends with Carmen, and now she'd done it again—open mouth, insert foot. She realized her mistake and found Carmen after class. She apologized over and over again. Carmen forgave her, but the relationship was never the same again.

Don't make the same mistake. Think before you blurt out your opinions. And if you blow it, ask for forgiveness as soon as possible.

Get along with each other, and forgive each other. If someone does wrong to you, forgive that person because the Lord forgave you. >>>>>>>>>>>>

## >> Colossians 3:13

It's Friday night, and you just got off work. You head over to a friends house to see what's up. Everyone is hanging around, playing PS2. You don't have to be home for a couple of hours, so you decide to stay. You sit down and start to chill when Hilary comes over and asks if she can talk with you for a minute. You head for a private place, and Hilary begins to tell you about how she has had a crush on you for a long time. She knew you really cared about your girlfriend, and she was really jealous. So she started some rumors about your girlfriend having two abortions. She thought it would break you up. But now she admits she was wrong and asks for your forgiveness.

What do you do? It's okay to be ticked—it was a really horrible thing for her to do. But, you've got to do three things.

Forgive. You've done horrible things too. Forgiveness is how we love each other.

Ask her to ask your girlfriend for forgiveness too.

Ask her to make your girlfriend's reputation clean again—admit to everyone that she lied about her.

Forgiveness needs to be given—especially when it's asked for. And wrongs need to be set right. But, even if she is unwilling to go that extra step and make things right you still need to do your part. Forgive.

245

When they had seen him, they told what the angels had said about this child. Everyone was amazed at what the shepherds said to them. But Mary treasured these things and continued to think about them. >>>>>>>>>>>>>>>>>>>>>>

Rachel was one of the best athletes to ever go through her school. She was on the swim team and an all-state volleyball player. But her real passion was skateboarding. She loved to ride and she was good. She was in the local newspaper a lot, and even got written up in several national magazines for her athletic abilities. She saved them all, along with all the notes she had received from people along the way. Then one day she was involved in a freak accident on her board. No one knew how she had wrecked, but she ended up paralyzed from the waist down.

She was angry and confused. Why did this happen to her? She blamed God for what had happened. It wasn't fair.

One day she was going to throw out all the articles and notes she had saved. Then she started reading some of them. She found a lot of them focused on her, not her athletics. As she thought about it, she realized that she was the same person, she just couldn't do some of the same things. She held on to the articles and notes, as well as some key verses from Psalms. They helped her through the down times.

Keep the encouraging notes and verses that you receive. They will come in handy when you are hurting or struggling.

And she gave birth to her first son. Because there were no rooms left in the inn, she wrapped the baby with pieces of cloth and laid him in a box where animals are fed. > > > > > > > > > > > > >

Do you really know the true story of Christmas? What kind of animals were present? What did the innkeeper say? Was there really a little drummer boy?

You wouldn't believe the things that people believe. Things that the Bible never talks about. Much of our Christmas theology is influenced by greeting cards and television. Take time, right now, to read all of Luke 2 and Matthew 1:18-2:12. Learn what really happened on the first Christmas.

Always give thanks to God the Father for everything, in the name of our Lord Jesus Christ. >>>>>>

What do you think of when you hear the word "Thanksgiving"? Turkey. Stuffed. Too much food. Pie. Pumpkins. Football. Sales. Parades. Being thankful?

It is one of the best holidays to celebrate. We get to eat way too much, watch tons of football, hit the stores to shop the big sales and check out all the big Christmas movie releases. We get together with friends and family to have fun and be thankful. For a Christian, that means a time to thank God for how He has blessed us. But tell me, why do we do it just one day out of the year?

I'm serious here. We need to take more time out to thank God. Why not have a Thanksgiving once a month? It doesn't have to be turkey and football. It could be tacos and chick flicks. It could happen in a variety of ways. The point is to set aside time to give God thanks—to recognize it more than just one day a year. Go ahead. Set aside a day next week and spend it thanking God. Make it a routine in your life.

> Jesus cried out in a loud voice, "Father, I give you my life." After Jesus said this, he died. 〉 〉 〉 〉 〉 〉

## >> Luke 23:46

We call it "Good Friday," but have you ever wondered what is so good about it? After all, it was a horrible day. It was the end of Jesus' trial. He was beaten beyond recognition and paraded through the town. People laughed at Him and spit on Him. After struggling up the hill, He met His executioners. They nailed His hands and feet to a rough, wooden cross and slammed it into the ground. When He got thirsty, they gave Him vinegar to drink. They laughed at Him as He hung there suffocating. With the flutter of His eyelashes, Jesus could have taken them all out. Yet He said little. Quietly He took what was given and died. It was a painful, miserable death. So why "Good Friday"?

I have to admit, I don't know the origins of the name. But I know this: There was something good about it. It was good that Jesus went through with it. His death was necessary. He had to die for the resurrection to take place. And without the resurrection, He was just another dead guy. It is good because it restored my relationship with God. The day might not have been good, but the results of the day were.

## >> Daniel 1:12-13

All of them are good things to be a part of. You are committed to band, football, baseball, water polo, working at Taco Bell, oh yeah, and church stuff. You like being involved in all the activities and your goal is to be a pro football player someday. You put a lot of time and energy into sports because your dad tells you that you can make lots of cash by being good at football. He puts you in all the camps, buys the nicest cleats, and even makes a personal highlight video to send to potential colleges he would like you to attend. You are involved in all the other sports to keep you in shape for football season and band because you love to play the drums. Taco Bell keeps the money in your pocket for dates.

When you hear of a water ski trip the church has planned, you really want to go, but your dad says no because it interferes with football camp. Even after almost begging, he still refuses. Your dad says he wants you involved in ministry, but his actions say that ministry can't interfere with football. What do you do?

Think of ways you can express to your parents that to you, ministry is more important than football. Make sure you are respectful. Somehow your priorities and those of your parents will have to line up. Begin discussing with them now how that can happen. Bottom line is you need to let them know how you feel.

## >> Ephesians 5:16

Did you see that? What about that? There's another one—did you see it?
You didn't? Were you looking? What are we talking about?
Opportunities. Most of the time we don't see them because we are too
busy doing something else. We fill our days with so much stuff that we
miss out on the things we might like or that really matter. You might be
the type of person who has trouble saying no to people when they ask
you to do something. People know that they can count on you. Your
schedule is filled so full that you miss out on chances for God to use you.
You're always "too busy." Simply put, you need to slow down.

Practice saying this word: "No." Try it again: "No." It's pretty easy to
say, and sometimes it needs to be said. We often have a schedule that is
too full to "do good." Just say no to the stuff that keeps you too busy to
do what God wants you to do. Maybe it is a night of work, or bowling
with your boyfriend, or even hanging out with your friends. Manage your
time to create more opportunities to "do good."

You have not seen Christ, but still you love him. You cannot see him now, but you believe in him. So you are filled with a joy that cannot be explained, a joy full of glory. And you are receiving the goal of your faith—the salvation of your souls. >>>>>>>>

What goals do you have for your life right now? Most students today have goals that are relationally based. That just means that you place a high value on relationships. Higher than the value you place on accomplishments. When your parents hear you want to be more involved in peoples' lives, they think about very specific accomplishments such as "state track champion" or "honor society." Honestly, goals can be whatever stretches you to go beyond where you are now, whether it's relationships or accomplishments.

Strive to be better by having some direction for what you want to accomplish over a selected amount of time. Peter said that the goal of our faith is "love, belief, and joy in Jesus." This develops as we get to know Jesus better, bringing "salvation to our souls." It is a great goal and not very rigid. It's relationally based. What is the goal of your faith? Once you figure that out, come up with three goals for the next three months that will help you get there. Remember to stretch yourself to go beyond where you are.

Goals:

1.

2.

3.

They said they were wise, but they became fools. They traded the glory of God who lives forever for the worship of idols made to look like earthly people, birds, animals, and snakes. > > > > > > > >

It is not wrong to have idols in your life. Did you know that? The issue is what we do with the idols.

Brenda was a huge fan of country music. She took voice lessons, played the guitar, and patterned her life after her favorite country music group. Everything the group did, Brenda did. Brenda would even draw fake tattoos on her ankle where the group had real ones. Brenda was completely obsessed with them, everything else in life was second to her country music. You think this sounds pathetic? I got news for you.

Brenda is not uncommon. It may not be country music; it could be a sport, movie, computer, celebrity, boy band, whatever. The problem is not liking these things, or even wanting to be like them. The problem is when we worship them. When we get so overtaken with them that we neglect and forget everything else. Our vision of life gets tunneled on one thing, and it isn't where it should be. God is the only person that you should be worshipping. You can idolize other things, but they should never rise above, or even come close to the level God is at in your life.

Maintain perspective; ALWAYS keep God number one. Look around your room; do you idolize what is represented in your room or do you worship it?

> With words an evil person can destroy a neighbor,
> but a good person will escape by being smart. >>

## >> Proverbs 11:9

What do you say to people? Do you usually encourage them or do you think you might be the type of person that is discouraging? Don't know? Try asking your friends, but be ready for a brutally honest answer.

I'll tell you what I see from my perspective. I listen to a lot of people and how they talk to others. Some people are encouraging and generally nice and people want to be around them. Then there are people who do nothing but cut everyone around them down. They might have some friends, but the friendships never go very deep. Why? Because there is a fear of being cut down about some personal issues that might get brought up. So people safeguard themselves from the negative type by keeping information to themselves. So, if you don't want to have any close friends, it's easy! Just put them down all the time. I guarantee that your friendships will start to fall apart.

If you have a friend doing it to you, put a stop to it. Tell them to quit. You can be nice, but let them know that you don't want to be talked to like that. There is too much in this world that tells us we don't measure up. We don't need to hear it from those we are close to.

Those who are stealing must stop stealing and start working. They should earn an honest living for themselves. Then they will have something to share with those who are poor. >>>>>>>>>>>>>>

Stealing has gotten so bad that stores are getting more and more high-tech to cut down on the incidents. Cameras are installed everywhere in stores to ensure that merchandise stays there until it's paid for—not just any cameras either, these cameras can read the names and numbers on sales receipts! They can focus that tightly.

But does that stop people from stealing? No. It has now turned into an art form. Some people can walk into a store with nothing and leave with hundreds of dollars worth of clothes. Remember, if it isn't yours, it isn't yours. Don't try and justify stealing by saying you should be able to have it even though you can't afford it. Find a way to earn and save your money. But don't steal.

You might have a problem with stealing. Maybe it has become a game to you, and you don't know how to stop. If that is you, get help by telling someone who can direct you where to go, like your pastor, counselor, or good friend.

If you see someone stealing, turn them in. You don't have to make it high profile, just tell a store clerk quietly and let them handle it. Don't let it go, otherwise you will keep paying for the dishonesty of other people.

## >> Nehemiah 5:13

Nobody likes to be lied to. And that is exactly how you feel when people don't keep their promises to you.

Maybe your dad sets up a week together and then, the night before you are to hook up with him, he calls and says that he isn't going to be able to come through. Or maybe that guy you like says that he will call you tomorrow. When six tomorrows go by, you realize that he just gave you a line and he never intends on calling you. Maybe these people didn't use the words "I promise," but taking them at their word is as good as a promise to you. It would be nice if we lived in a perfect world, but we don't and there will be people that will let us down.

Turn the tables now and think about when you let others down. How could you have prevented it? If your thoughts are "Well I never promised, I just said I would try," remember, people take you at face value.

Try this for an exercise: Every time you count change from your pocket, ask the question of whether people can count on you. Then live your life in a way that people can, holding to your word.

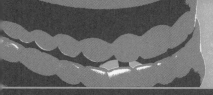

"I know what you do, that you are not hot or cold. I wish that you were hot or cold! But because you are lukewarm—neither hot, nor cold—I am ready to spit you out of my mouth." >>>>>>>>>>>>

Every time you wash your face, clean the dishes, take a shower, or brush your teeth (assuming you do at least one of these regularly) it should be a reminder. A reminder for you to examine where you are in your spiritual life. Is it hot, meaning are you actively burning up your world for the cause of Christ? Or is it cold, meaning that God makes no difference in your life whatsoever. Either way, own up to where you're at, because you don't want to be lukewarm, caught in the middle. What does lukewarm mean? It could mean that you are really cold but try to sell yourself as hot. More than likely it means that you can't decide where you are with God. You like the "fire insurance" that God gives, but the rules of being a Christian drag you down too much.

One thing is for sure when you read this passage, God wants you to take your spiritual temperature. What is it? Hot or cold? If you want to ride the middle some more, remember this: God gets sick of people who are lukewarm, sick to the point of throwing up. Go stand in front of your bathroom faucet and decide, are you hot or cold?

Now, everything has been heard, so I give my final advice: Honor God and obey his commands, because this is all people must do. God will judge everything, even what is done in secret, the good and the evil. >>>>>>>>>>>>>>>>>>

What would you do if your mom gave you a thousand dollars and told you to go spend it on whatever you wanted? She never gave you any boundaries, she just said go out, spend the money, and enjoy yourself. So you do. With a little scratch in your hand you go and have the time of your life for an entire weekend. You find someone to buy you and your friends some alcohol. You buy more food than you can eat and end up throwing a lot of it away. You and your friends party hearty. It was a fun weekend, at least you think it was.

On Monday morning your mom comes into your room to tell you why she gave you the money and let you go. She wanted to see if you had learned all the lessons of life you need to know. She wanted to see how you would react to the money. She now wants to know what you did with it, because that will determine whether or not she is going to make you pay it back. You feel a big knot in your stomach and wish you had the weekend to do over again.

Our life will be the same way. The writer of Ecclesiastes said you can "eat, drink, and be merry, but remember you will be judged for all that you do." How will God look at your life when you stand before Him?

## >> Revelation 3:17

"You say, 'I am rich, and I have become wealthy and do not need anything.' But you do not know that you are really miserable, pitiful, poor, blind, and naked." >>>>>>>>>>>>>>>>>>>>>>>>

Pride can be a terrible thing. It can trick us into believing that we are completely self-sufficient, that we don't need anything or anybody. Pride makes you look at those around you and feel sorry that they don't get to live your great life. Pride says that you have all you want and need. God doesn't even fit into your universe, and why should He? You don't need him either. As a matter of fact you don't need anybody, because you can do it yourself. If people ask, you tell them that you are more than able.

What pride doesn't do is allow you to see yourself for who you really are. It doesn't admit that we all have needs in our life, no matter what our status is. It ignores the fact that we are failures that need a God who can pull us along when we can't do it ourselves.

It is okay to admit that we have needs, because it causes us to accept love from others. Think for a second about what you really need in this life. Be honest. Have you told God about that yet?

259

Then God led Abram outside and said. "Look at the sky. There are so many stars you cannot count them. Your descendants also will be too many to count." >>>>>>>>>>>>>>>>>>>>>>>>>>>

Find a warm clear night and go outside. Find a place you can lay down and look at the stars. Lay there for fifteen minutes trying to think of nothing except God. It is harder than it sounds. As you direct your thoughts toward God, listen to what He is saying to you.

Abraham listened, do you?

> "Be strong and brave. Don't be afraid of them and don't be frightened, because the LORD your God will go with you. He will not leave you or forget you."

## >> Deuteronomy 31:6

> >>>>>>>>>>>>>>>>>>>>>>>>>>>>

Tomorrow is the day. The last two weeks of anticipation have been creating quite a bit of stress in Carrie's life. Tomorrow she will present her oral argument in her speech class on the topic of abortion. Carrie believes that all abortions are wrong, no exceptions. A life is a life, even if that life is in the womb of a woman who doesn't want it. She knows that the majority of her class thinks that her views are very old-fashioned. Carrie doesn't push her point of view on anyone, but she will always let you know where she stands if you ask her.

She can hardly sleep the night before because she knows the attack that's going to ensue after her speech. After she presents her case, she will then have to defend it in front of everyone. "What if I confuse everyone, or mess up really bad?" These are the thoughts that keep going through her head.

Carrie can't calm down until she remembers a talk on courage that she heard at church a while ago. She finds the passage her pastor referred to: Deuteronomy 31:6. Before class Carrie writes the verse on top of her paper and it helps her not get scared as she stands in front of everyone and tells them her beliefs.

Everyone God made is good, and nothing should be refused if it is accepted with thanks. >>>>>>

Julie can't believe the way she looks. When she checks herself out in the mirror, she is horrified by what she sees. At 5'6" and 105 pounds she is still way too fat. She complains about how she looks to her mom, and her mom tells her she is being dumb. Still, Julie can't get beyond what she sees. Most people tell her she looks great and so thin, but Julie doesn't buy it.

Julie's mom starts noticing that Julie is eating less and is quick to get excused from the table. She thinks it is just a phase and that Julie will get over it. "Every girl hates her body at some point in her life," she thinks. One night she hears Julie getting sick in the bathroom. She goes in, and Julie confesses that she has a problem. Julie admits to sticking a toothbrush down her throat to make herself throw up after she eats. It started innocently enough, but now it seems out of control. Julie needs help. She knows this could kill her.

It's easy to say "be satisfied with who you are." But sometimes we aren't. If you know a Julie or are a Julie, find help. Call this number to get help today: 1-847-831-3438.

## >> Genesis 4:3-4a

Later, Cain brought some food from the ground as a gift to God. Abel brought the best parts from some of the firstborn of his flock. ›››››››

Ellen could draw really well. No, it is better to say that she was an artist. When she put colors on paper and canvas, they seemed to come alive. She wasn't limited to drawing just one thing either, she could draw anything she wanted. Landscapes, people, you name it, and she could bring it to life through her pencil or her paints. She had a gift.

One day her pastor approached her about doing some artwork for an upcoming series of talks on the twenty-third Psalm. He wanted to know if Ellen could put something together that would help illustrate what the psalm means from several points of view. Ellen agreed to do it, then put the project on the back burner.

The day before the pictures were due at the church, Ellen read the psalm and drew some quick sketches. They looked okay, but they weren't her best work. She hung them in the church and walked away.

The thing is, they weren't just "church pictures." They were offerings—an act of worship offered to God. God wants our best, not our leftovers. What are you giving Him?

On the seventh day they got up at dawn and marched around the city, just as they had on the days before. But on that day they marched around the city seven times. >>>>>>>>>>>>>>>

Don't you hate feeling bored? Doing something that feels like it has no purpose at all? Doing something you've done a zillion times before?

The Hebrews must have felt the same way when God told them to walk around the walls of Jericho every day for seven days. Then on the last day, they had to walk around seven times. You know they were thinking, "Oh great, we get to walk around this stupid wall again." Maybe they thought it, but they never said it. There is no record of complaint from them, probably because they knew the purpose of what they were doing. God was going to do something big, they just had to do their part and walk.

The next time you start feeling like you've heard or seen it all before, stop and think about what God is trying to show or tell you—no doubt it's something new. You might be surprised to see the walls come down in your life.

"So, all the people of Israel should know this truly: God has made Jesus—the man you nailed to the cross—both Lord and Christ." When the people heard this, they felt guilty and asked Peter and the other apostles, "What shall we do?" > > > > > > >

What convicts you? Maybe you're the type of person who never feels convicted. Anything goes as long as it doesn't hurt you. You can do, say, and think whatever you want. As long as you like it, it must be okay. But there is a problem with this attitude. There are sin issues involved. For example, not telling the truth is lying, and lying is a sin. Some people have no convictions about it, but that doesn't mean it's okay. Bottom line is that there is no "okay" sin ever mentioned in the Bible. Sin is always wrong.

Convictions act like an alarm for our sin. They make us aware of when we are about to sin or have sinned. You don't have to beat yourself up over it. Simply work at not allowing sin to screw up your relationship with Him. Listen to your convictions. If God is behind them, they will lead you down the right road.

"From the east to the west I will be honored among the nations. Everywhere they will bring incense and clean offerings to me, because I will be honored among the nations," says the LORD All-Powerful.

> > > > > > > > > > > > > > > > > > > > > > > > > >

How far are you willing to go for God? How many miles and how remote a location will you go to serve God? What kind of conditions will you allow yourself to live in to let others know what God is doing in your life? Not a trip for the sake of a trip, not a vacation, not a sight-seeing adventure, simply a mission to share God.

There are lots of mission opportunities available every year. Check them out by looking up local ministry websites. Don't sit back and wish you could go, don't let money be the issue (trust God), don't worry about conditions (you will be taken care of—enjoy the adventure), put aside all excuses and go.

If we want to see God's name honored by every nation, we need to go and tell the other nations about Him. Look today at what's available and plan on going. If you have gone, go again. There are still lots of people who need to hear.

Teach older men to be self-controlled, serious, wise, strong in faith, in love, and in patience. >>>>>

Every time Dena came home, it seemed that her mom was waiting for her. Dena's mom was under a lot of stress being a single, working mom with four kids. Dena always felt like she could never live up to what her mom wanted. It started to become a ritual: She would come home and a fight would begin. Mom didn't like anything Dena was doing, and she was releasing her stress on her. Her mom couldn't hang on to her emotions when she got irritated. She would always lose her temper full-out. Dena couldn't handle it and lost her temper with her mom. A couple of times it got to the point where the two of them punched each other.

Dena believed she would do something she would regret if she didn't get control of her temper. So she went out and bought a "super ball." You know, a little rubber ball that bounces really high. She always kept it with her because she realized her temper was like that ball. As long as it was in her hand it was controlled. As soon as she let it go it took some work to gain control of it again. Just slowing down, gaining some self control of her own temper helped Dena, and in turn her mom blew up less often.

## >> Romans 12:2

Do not change yourselves to be like the people of this world, but be changed within by a new way of thinking. Then you will be able to decide what God wants for you: you will know what is good and pleasing to him and what is perfect. >> >> >> >>

It has been said that "changed lives change lives." It is true. You can watch it happen. People notice a life that changes. When you see a person change the way they live, the way they relate to others, or improve their attitude, it does something. It can be the spark that starts a red hot fire of change in a whole bunch of people! See someone change and you almost can't help but want to change as well. It just looks so cool to see someone's fire light up.

Do you want to see your church or group of friends start to really change? Watch someone who isn't a Christian become one. You might have to share your faith with them (yeah—that can feel scary) but it'll be worth it. The changing life of one person can inspire the changing lives of too many people to count.

If you want to see the lives around you change, you might have to change your own life first. What might be something you need to change in your life?

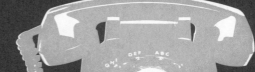

Everything you do or say should be done to obey Jesus your Lord. And in all you do, give thanks to God the Father through Jesus. >>>>>>>>>>

>> **Colossians 3:17**

There are four common responses I hear regarding why people don't like church or youth groups. "It's boring," "It's irrelevant," "It doesn't do anything for me," and "I don't have any friends there."

Sometimes church is boring. I have sat through my share of boring services. The problem with this argument is that what is boring to me may not be boring to the person next to me. I need to be patient and work at listening to what God wants me to hear.

It might feel irrelevant, but again that's subjective. As you listen and watch services and programs, think of creative ways that you can make them relevant to your world.

Doesn't do anything for you? Is that really the truth, or have you put up a wall so nothing gets to you? God's always available to make an impact; are you inviting Him to do it?

And if your friends don't come to church, then bring 'em! Or make new friends there.

Church can be everything you want it to be. Sometimes you have to be the one that gets it going though. Be part of the solution and not the problem.

He said, "You people understand that it is against our law for Jewish people to associate with or visit anyone who is not Jewish. But God has shown me that I should not call any person 'unholy' or 'unclean.'" >>>>>>>>>>>>>>>>>>>>>>>

What's the deal with racism? I mean, who decides that one person is better than another because of the color of his skin? We think we've gotten over it all, but it's still here. We all have our moments of pride when we explain something kinda weird, "There was this white girl . . ." "These Hispanic guys . . ." "A Middle Eastern woman . . . ." Why not just "a girl," "some guys," or "a woman"?

It's subtle, but it's there. We don't feel quite comfortable going to that church 'cause it's mainly black. We don't want to go that route to the party, at least not alone, 'cause we're not sure it's "safe."

The Bible says we shouldn't consider anyone else less than us, based on race or anything. We should hang out with them, be friends with them. And not because we want them to be our "project," our "good deed."

This week make a new friend—a bud, one of the guys, an equal.

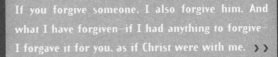

If you forgive someone, I also forgive him. And what I have forgiven—if I had anything to forgive—I forgave it for you, as if Christ were with me. >>

I am probably a little more sensitive than most to things that are considered evil. Not just bad, but satanic evil. I loved the movie *Ghostbusters*, but now I can't watch it. The way they talk about occult stuff really bothers me. You might think I'm being freakishly conservative, but these are my convictions. I have them because I believe that if we let our guard down, Satan can try to capitalize on our lives. If you look at images of evil, they are next to impossible to get out of your mind.

The next time you feel scared about something, even just a little, you'll remember those images and get freaked. At that point, Satan knows he has you, and he can use the element of fear on you however he wants. It is one of the ways that Satan tries to defeat us. Paul talks about it in the book of Ephesians.

Don't get paranoid and look for Satan or demons behind every rock that turns over. Do like Peter says in his first letter and "stand strong in your faith" (1 Peter 5:9). Avoid evil if you can, and always look for ways to do the good things in life that please God.

271

Finally, all of you should be in agreement, understanding each other, loving each other as family, being kind and humble. >>>>>>>>>

>> i Peter 3:8

Y'all can never decide what to do. Everyone has their own opinion—swimming ("No way am I going to put on a swimsuit!"), movies (drama, comedy, romance), ultimate frisbee ("No, I hate getting sweaty"). So, you end up just sitting around at McDonalds wondering what you're going to do. Finally, you all go home because it's your curfew.

You really like your friends, but you guys waste a lot of time trying to agree on something. Sometimes you'll just have to sacrifice—do something you don't really love one week for the sake of being with your friends. When they call to see if you want to see a movie don't ask, "Which one?" right off the bat. They'll think being entertained is more important to you than hanging with them.

Be honest with your friends, and give a little. They'll really appreciate it.

## >> Romans 10:2-3

I can say this about them: They really try to follow God, but they do not know the right way. Because they did not know the way that God makes people right with him, they tried to make themselves right in their own way. So they did not accept God's way of making people right. >>>>>>>>>>>>>>

Salvation, that big word that means "God saved us from our sin through Jesus," is the only thing that gets us into heaven. You probably know this, so let's say it again. Salvation is the only thing we need to get into heaven.

Now I agree that there are things that go along with salvation. Jesus talked a lot about the way that we should live our life once we are saved. But it's funny to me that there are some who think there are extra requirements for being a Christian, stuff like: You can't listen to secular music, you have to go on a mission trip, you can only watch "G" rated movies, and certain words are wrong to say (like "crap").

Maybe these are or aren't the type of activities that you engage in, but they have no bearing on your salvation. You might use words that your parents don't like—so maybe you need to evaluate your words—but they won't destroy your relationship with God. Nothing can. There's nothing in the Bible that says it can. In this case, disobeying your parents is the bigger issue, and probably the one you need to address.

Let's become more focused on the things that are important to Jesus and less focused on the things that were important to the Pharisees.

> "I have filled Bezalel with the Spirit of God and have given him the skill, ability, and knowledge to do all kinds of work. >>>>>>>>>>>>>>>>>

## >> Exodus 31:3

Think today about God's spirit, and how He's living inside you. Try to visualize it. Think about the skills, abilities, and knowledge that you have because of that.

## >> 2 Corinthians 7:1

Dear friends, we have these promises from God, so we should make ourselves pure—free from anything that makes body or soul unclean. We should try to become holy in the way we live, because we respect God.  >>>>>>>>>>>>>>>>>>>>>>>>>>

When I read verses like this, I try to think through how we define "holy." When you get down to it, holiness really means to be set apart. Huh? Well, let's say you pick up a dozen donuts for your Bible study, and the bakery only had one chocolate covered donut left (your favorite). You ask the guy to put that one in a bag (for you) and the rest in the box for the other guys. You've "set apart" that donut—it's the one you want. As Christians, we are set apart for God.

We're also set apart in a different way—we have a particular mission here on earth. God had a purpose in creating us. When the director of the FBI picks his top agent to go alone on a special mission, that guy is set apart. So, let's look at ourselves. In light of your surroundings (friends, family, school, etc.) how are you set apart? What makes you so different? What's your mission?

Setting ourselves apart doesn't mean that we don't interact in the world around us. Look at the life of Jesus. He had a vital ministry, even though He was a holy man. It means that the way God wants us to live is different than the way the world lives. Can you see a difference?

## >> Esther 1:10-11

You've probably never used anyone, have you? Never manipulated a situation to get what you want. Everyone you know in your life is taken for who they are, and there are never any strings attached, right?

I knew when I was growing up that some of my "friends" were only friends with me because my family had a swimming pool. I wanted to be popular in school, so I didn't care if people liked me just for my pool. I wanted to hang out with the "in" crowd.

I can't get too mad or upset about it. I am sure that I did it to someone else. I probably befriended someone who had a sister that I thought was hot. I think I developed a friendship with a guy from another church so I could go on one of that church's retreats. It isn't right to do, but I think if we look deep inside ourselves, we all are guilty of using someone in some way or another. It doesn't have to be friends; it can be siblings, parents, teachers, or you name it.

You don't have to use or be used. Be real and authentic in all your relationships. Be yourself because no one else can do it as well as you can.

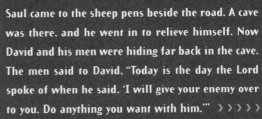

## >> 1 Samuel 24:3-4a

Saul came to the sheep pens beside the road. A cave was there, and he went in to relieve himself. Now David and his men were hiding far back in the cave. The men said to David, "Today is the day the Lord spoke of when he said, 'I will give your enemy over to you. Do anything you want with him.'" >>>>>

I have always loved the stories from the life of David.

I like this one for two reasons. As a kid I thought it was funny that the Bible had a story about going to the bathroom. Now that I am older, I appreciate David's patience with God.

No matter how rotten of a leader Saul turned out to be, David would not allow himself to take matters into his own hands. David had plenty of opportunities to kill Saul or have some of his men do it, but David allowed God to deal with Saul. David went about, not leading a revolt, but providing protection for himself and Israel.

God said He would take care of Saul, and David had the patience to let Him. When things feel like they are bad, let God have control. Hold back and be patient, letting Him do what He needs to. He has run our world for a long time. If He needs our help, He will let us know. In other words—give situations some time to see if they work out.

I don't care about my own life. The most important thing is that I complete my mission, the work that the Lord Jesus gave me—to tell people the Good News about God's grace. >>>>>>>>>>>>>

Anyone can take part in a race. No matter what stage of life you are in or how disabled you feel you might be, you will still be in the race of life. There are many stages that you go through, and it is not enough that you are in the race—you want to finish at the top.

It gets too easy to quit when things don't go our way. Hey—it's easy to do well when things are going well. The real test of our character is how well we do when we have problems. Do you quit when stuff gets hard or do you put your head up and look straight ahead at where you want to get to? After one race is finished, do you find another to run?

Please don't just run your life aimlessly, not knowing where you're going. It is okay to be undecided about what you want to do for a career. My point is to know whom you live for. Don't let your life pass by as you try to find purpose and meaning. You can find your purpose and meaning through God and what He says in the Bible.

When you look back at your life, look at all the "races" you've competed in. In those, did you merely finish or did you finish well?

Have you ever done something incredible that no one saw? Maybe you kicked a basketball into the basket from a full court away. It could be that your car tipped up on two wheels as you swerved to miss hitting a deer. Perhaps you scored a million points on your new PS2 game, only to have your little sister accidentally erase it. You were so proud of your accomplishment, but there were no witnesses!

It could be that you like it that way. You might have done something stupid that you don't want anyone to know about, like checking the tip of a spray paint can and spraying yourself in the face. How about tripping over nothing, just the carpet? Many of us have done things that we would rather not have anyone else know about.

Guess what? God sees everything: good, bad, stupid, and incredible. No matter what, He is always proud of you and will always point you in the right direction. He is the proud father of a daughter who goes to the plate and strikes out. The beaming dad of a son who forgets a line in his school play. He sees it all, and though He doesn't like all that you do, He is still proud of who you are.

> Some other seed fell on good ground where it grew and produced a crop. Some plants made a hundred times more, some made sixty times more, and some made thirty times more. >>>>>>>>>>>>>

What kind of dirt-bag are you?

Jesus made a point to tell the people around Him about the value of good dirt. Dirt that had too many rocks in it caused the seed that was planted to sprout too quickly and die too soon. In translation, this is a person who comes to faith in Jesus, maybe in an emotionally charged moment, but they never get grounded in what they believe. It looked good for a time but quickly changed back.

Maybe your dirt is full of weeds. The weeds choke the plant and keep it from growing to its full potential. Translation: the person that has so many commitments in their life that they choke out God. These other weeds might be good plants but not when they take us away from God.

Last, there was good soil. Seeds were planted in it and grew well. These thriving and growing Christians are fully rooted and growing in their faith. They love God and it shows.

So, what kind of dirt-bag are you? Keep a nice, healthy plant in your room to remind you about where your relationship is with God.

Those who carried materials did their work with one hand and carried a weapon with the other. Each builder wore his sword at his side as he worked. >>>>>>>>>>>>>>>>>>>>>>>>>>>>

Jenn was busy with so many other things that studying wasn't high on her priority list. She had student government, her job at the GAP, a freelance photography hobby, and her friends. The test coming up in algebra probably wouldn't be that hard anyway, so she kept putting off the studying. The night before the test, she never quite got to the algebra, but Jenn had a brilliant idea. She has always had a great relationship with God, so she decided to ask God to help her get a good grade. God would obviously understand how important these other distractions were. After her short prayer, Jenn closed her math book and went to sleep.

The next day Jenn went into the test confident she would do well. God would be with her, so how could she fail? Well, she did fail.

At first Jenn was really mad at God for letting her down. But after a while she realized that it was her own fault. She hadn't made an effort. Look at the passage in Nehemiah again. We see that they worked with their swords close by. They did this even after they prayed for God's protection. Did you ever think that the sword might be the protection? God will do His part always, but we need to do ours as well.

And all need to be made right with God by his grace, which is a free gift. They need to be made free from sin through Jesus Christ. >>>>>>

It is very easy to get caught up in the ugliness of the world today. Just watch the news on television and you will see all sorts of evil acts from people who have little or no regard for others. On any given day you can hear the news of senseless murders, terrorist bombings, kidnappings, missing persons, road rage, and every other crime known to man. I know for myself, it is very easy to form a judgment against the people who are accused and/or convicted of these terrible crimes. I have my own ideas about what should be done with these people, and I am sad to admit that some of those thoughts are not very God-honoring. The thing that helps me keep all the events of our world and communities in perspective is this: The sins of my life put Jesus on the cross just the same as the sins of these other people. Mine may not be of the same magnitude, but they are sins just the same.

We can rest in the forgiveness of our sins. We know that God is faithful to forgive when we ask for it. We all need a God who loved us so much that He provided a way to Himself through His Son. Live your life in a way that honors what God did for you.

Jesus said, "Anyone who begins to plow a field but keeps looking back is of no use in the kingdom of God." >>>>>>>>>>>>>>>>>>>>>>>>>>

Emma had just won a starting spot on the varsity softball team, and she was only a freshman. Getting to play at such a high level meant a higher time commitment. She wouldn't be able to be as involved at church anymore. She spent so much time working out that by the time she got home, ate, and did her homework she was wiped out and went to bed. No time for reading her Bible before sleep like in the past. Along with the status of being on the varsity team came invitations to weekend parties. Emma was flattered that she got invited—none of her friends had!

Life seemed to be good. Emma's parents noticed that the more time she spent in softball, the less time she had for God. They let her know their concern. Emma let them know that there would be plenty of time for God when she got older. Besides, she still loved God, she just didn't have as much time for him as she used to.

God wants us to move forward in our relationship with Him. There will be obstacles that take our focus off Him, and God will always let it be our choice—we choose how much we want to follow Him. He wants our whole, devoted heart for Himself, not the leftovers.

## >> Exodus 4:10

But Moses said to the LORD, "Please, Lord, I have never been a skilled speaker. Even now, after talking to you, I cannot speak well. I speak slowly and can't find the best words." >>>>>>>>>>>>>

You can't see it, but everyone has got one. It's not physical, but it can keep you from moving. It's our "comfort zone." We get to the point where we just don't feel adequate enough to move beyond where we are. We won't go talk to someone new at our school or work. We are unwilling to ask that "special" someone out. It keeps us from trying out for the golf team, because we don't want to be embarrassed by how bad our game is.

You know what? It is much easier to sit and do nothing than to try something new and fail. And unfortunately, you'll never expand yourself if you don't try something new. You may even look back someday and think, "Man, I wish I would have tried that." Don't end up that way. Break through your comfort zone. Extend yourself to someone who looks lonely. Try a new sport that you have never tried before but you think might be fun. Ask out that person you've always wanted to date. They might say no, then again, they might say yes. Go ahead, as long as it isn't sin, try it.

But the snake said to the woman. "You will not die. God knows that if you eat the fruit from that tree, you will learn about good and evil and you will be like God!" >>>>>>>>>>>>>>>>>>>>>>>>>

It all comes down to what I want. If I want to make the lives of everyone around me miserable, so be it. It's my world and everyone else is just a part of it. *Here are the Rules of Selfishness:*

Believe that you are the most important person not only in your own life, but also in the lives of everyone around you.

Make sure you get noticed at all costs. Remember that everything is about you.

Always talk about yourself and your accomplishments. Ignore the people around you.

Live your life so that everyone notices you are only concerned about you.

Let the people around you know that their feelings are not important.

All kidding aside, selfishness is a sure way to make people not want to be around you. Jesus always taught about meeting the needs of the people around us. That is what life in the body of Christ is all about.

When Adam and Eve sinned in the garden of Eden, it was the sin of selfishness. She thought that she could become like God. Don't fall into the same type of trap. Think of others first, then yourself.

285

So Potiphar arrested Joseph and put him into the prison where the king's prisoners were put. And Joseph stayed there in the prison. But the Lord was with Joseph and showed him kindness and caused the prison warden to like Joseph. >>>>>>>

You think *you* have bad days! Look at the life of Joseph in the book of Genesis! He had one perpetual bad day! He was constantly being held against his will. His brothers sold him, a trusted boss turned on him, and he ended up in prison in a foreign land. You would think that Joseph would have said, "Punt God! Who needs this in life?" There is a part of us that really wouldn't have blamed Joseph if he had! But he didn't. He didn't allow external circumstances to affect his relationship with his God. There came a point, and we don't know when it was, that Joseph must have realized a very important principle: If you can't see tomorrow, make today count.

Everywhere Joseph went, he made today count. He didn't wait and hope he would be taken care of, he lived his life with God as a vital part of it, every day. We don't know if Joseph sulked about his circumstances, but we don't read about it.

How do you handle adversity? Do you drop God when things don't go your way or do you not worry about tomorrow and make today count?

>> 1 Corinthians 14:3

But those who prophesy are speaking to people to give them strength, encouragement, and comfort.

>>>>>>>>>>>>>>>>>>>>>>>>>>>>>>

One night Jon was flipping through the channels on TV when he stumbled on to some of the religious stuff that's on at night. The program was interviewing a woman who claimed to have the gift of prophecy. As she was explaining how these gifts were confirmed to her, Jon was a little skeptical. Next, she began to predict the death and destruction of the world. How systematically, everyone would be burned alive for their faith, that terror would rain down throughout the world, and that for $44.95 you could be saved by purchasing space in a special bunker she had set up.

Jon remained skeptical of what she said. It seemed like she was just playing on the fears of people to make a buck. He was pretty sure that a lot of people would have the bejeebers scared out of them and buy into her plot. Jon turned the channel.

The Bible makes it clear in the New Testament that we should find strength, encouragement, and comfort in prophetic words, not fear. Think about it.

>> Romans 8:39

Nothing above us, nothing below us, nor anything else in the whole world will ever be able to separate us from the love of God that is in Christ Jesus our Lord. >>>>>>>>>>>>>>>>>>>>

Absolutely nothing. Nothing, nothing, nothing. That is what can separate us from God's love. God's love will always be there for us. He will never take it away. His love will be in our very presence every day of our lives, even if we try to get away from it. So lets put it into perspective. Let's check out some of the things that can't separate us from God's love: Mom and Dad, boy/girlfriend, school, job, pain, death, football, Tom Green, fear, cousins, friends, boredom, Marilyn Manson, computers, busy signals, mad dogs, country music, Islamic extremists, movies, and on and on.

Now let's think about what can separate us from God's love: nothing.

There may be times when you feel like God doesn't love you, but in those times go back to this verse and be assured that He does. Feelings can lie to you and trusting a lie can bring disastrous results. Maybe you should get an old plastic pop bottle and take off the label. Use a blank mailing label to put on the outside that says "contents inside bottle can separate me from God's love."

Then Joseph had another dream, and he told his brothers about it also. He said, "Listen, I had another dream. I saw the sun, moon, and eleven stars bowing down to me." Joseph also told his father about this dream, but his father scolded him. >>>>>>>>>>>>>>>>>>>>>>>>>>>>>>>>

Nobody likes arrogance. We might be able to tolerate it for a while, but in the end it is really irritating to be around someone who thinks very highly of themselves. They might like to look in the mirror a lot, primp up, and strut around hoping the whole world will see how great they are. And they constantly talk about how great they think they are. That was Joseph. His arrogance was so bad, he even irritated his parents. Joseph was clueless that he was being arrogant. It had become a way of life for him to feel over-important, and he bought into it.

Do you notice when you're arrogant? Most people don't notice their own arrogance because they are so focused on how they look or how cool they are. They forget to see how they look to others. Look at your life through the eyes of someone else. Try it. How do your friends see you? What about your parents? Teachers? Church? Now, what can you do to make that perception better?

Samuel said, "You acted foolishly! You haven't obeyed the command of the LORD your GOD. If you had obeyed him, the Lord would have made your kingdom continue in Israel always." >>>>>>

Does God use fools? Sure. But he doesn't want to use people who act foolishly. Is there a difference? Yes. We are all fools. We do dumb stuff all the time. You might be the type of person who always trips getting out of a car. Or maybe you're the type who can never remember to zip up your fly. How about when you laugh and drink something at the same time? Does the drink come out your nose? See, in some way at some time we all look like fools, and it is usually something we can laugh about and move on.

But it is an entirely different issue to be foolish. It makes God angry when we are foolish, especially with the ministry He has entrusted to us. When Jesus left this earth, He gave the work of the church to us, and we need to be responsible with it. While still understanding we are fools, we are not to be foolish with His kingdom. Don't lead people astray, making them believe something that isn't true. Look always to help and to love the people around you. Encourage and invite everyone you know to develop and deepen their relationship with God.

God has entrusted His kingdom into your hands! Take it seriously. Don't be foolish with your responsibility.

You have saved me from all my troubles, and I have seen my enemies defeated. > > > > > > > > > > > >

The coffee business is a tough world, and when a local coffee shop announced that it was hiring ten new employees, you wanted to be one, because the shop is the coolest in town.

You wait and wait by the phone, but no call comes. You feel like a total idiot. You worked really hard to get hired there. Somehow though, you didn't make it. You told everyone that you were going to be working there. Now how are you going to face them? What about the car you've been dreaming about and needed this money to buy?

In the midst of this emotion you make a vow never to buy coffee there again. You won't even go near the place. That'll teach them! But later, after you've had time to cool down, you realize that is a totally stupid idea. Everybody hangs there. You like it. You want to go there. Instead, make the vow that you will not allow yourself to get that upset over something you cannot control. For all you know, the manager hired his ten best friends and it had nothing to do with you, so let it go.

Just maybe God is leading you somewhere else. Pray now and ask Him to show you what He wants you to do.

## >> Matthew 14:29-31

Jesus said, "Come." And Peter left the boat and walked on the water to Jesus. But when Peter saw the wind and the waves, he became afraid and began to sink. He shouted, "Lord, save me!" Immediately Jesus reached out his hand and caught Peter. Jesus said, "Your faith is small. Why did you doubt?" >>>>>>>>>>>>>>>>

You are feeling really torn about this decision. They are all nice guys, but maybe it's not the right kind of band for you to drum with. They play all of this dark rock and goth music that you kind of like, but don't know if it is where you want to be. None of the other band members are Christians, and the kind of music they play is a little scary. Normally you would never consider playing with these guys, but two things stick out right now.

First, there is no other band asking you to play. Second, you really feel God is leading you to play here. You're not sure exactly why, but it probably has to do with the fact that they are non-Christians. You accept the offer to play. You make your personal, spiritual convictions clear from the start, and keep bringing them up at rehearsals. After playing together for about two months, they bring in a very anti-God song. They know how you feel about it but think this is the right direction for the band.

Are you going to sink or swim? What issues of your faith will you step up for and which will you crumble against?

Dead flies can make even perfume stink. In the same way, a little foolishness can spoil wisdom.

>>>>>>>>>>>>>>>>>>>>>>>>>>>>>>>>>

The grades you get are decent, usually making the honor roll. People say you have street smarts and "handle yourself well with others." You like to think of yourself as intelligent. That's why it is so weird what you did last Friday night.

You just dropped your friends off after a night of hanging out and causing trouble at the bowling alley. Nothing bad, just your own style of power bowling, throwing the balls down the lane really fast. You were all alone and decided to see what your dad's car could really do.

The road home is fairly straight with only one slight turn. As you head down the straightaway, you see how fast the engine will really go. It reaches 100 mph. You see the curve coming ahead, but now it's coming faster than you're used to. You panic. The car slides sideways. As you try to regain control, you hit the gravel and end up sliding into the grass field beside the road.

Whew! No damage to the car. You just drive away. As you get closer to home you realize how dumb a stunt it was. It could have been very ugly, and for what? When you get behind the wheel, drive smart. Put something yellow on your key chain to remind you to be smart when you drive.

Try hard to live right and to have faith, love and peace, together with those who trust in the Lord from pure hearts. >>>>>>>>>>>>>>>>>>

>> 2 Timothy 2:22b

You might be the type of girl that dreams of a Prince Charming. You have seen all of the latest chick flicks, and inside of your mind you constantly imagine the scene when Mr. Perfect sweeps you off your feet. You honestly feel like you can't see enough of these movies or think about it too much. You always get the new *Bride* magazine, and you dream about your wedding day.

You watch your friends with their boyfriends and think about how lucky they are to have such great guys in their life. The guys you go out with never measure up. They burp at the table, only want to watch action movies, and like to show off all the time. It is never like it is in the movies. Most of the time the guys you date never make it to date number two, because you have lost interest so soon.

These guys may never make the standard you set. The reality is that most guys have never seen those movies and have no idea what you're looking for. You can't expect them to be something they aren't or don't want to be. So what do you do?

Make a list of qualities you think any guy you date has to have, things like he's gotta be a Christian, he needs to be funny, he can't burp in public, and so on. If a guy asks you out and he makes the list, go with him. But when you're out, don't think about the list. Think about getting to know him. Don't try to make him larger than life. Give the guy a chance to be himself first.

## >> 2 Corinthians 6:14

You are not the same as those who do not believe. So do not join yourselves to them. Good and bad do not belong together. Light and darkness cannot share together. >>>>>>>>>>>>>>>>>>>>>>>>

You are the greatest couple in the school. You have been dating for a little over a month and you know you are in love. When you go to your small group meeting, your leader asks you what the Bible has to say about cults. You know all of this and you are ready. You respond with your standard answer of "Well, cults don't use the Word of God." Your leader points out that you are not completely right. Some cults do use the Bible. You are again ready with an answer, "Well, those people just use the parts of the Bible that fit their life. They pick and choose. They don't take the Book as a whole."

Your leader switches subjects and asks you if, as Christians, you believe it is okay to date non-Christians. You say, "Sure, what will it hurt?" Then your leader reads this passage from 2 Corinthians. You think about it and decide this verse doesn't apply—it was meant for the people at the time it was written. You're back peddling because your steady isn't a Christian. "Oh," your leader says. "So how are you different from those cults?" Ouch. It hurts, but it makes you think. Who are you joined to?

The wicked draw their swords and bend their bows to kill the poor and helpless, to kill those who are honest. >>>>>>>>>>>>>>>>>>>>>>>>>>>

Admit it, you messed up. Don't try to pass it off as no big deal. Anytime we do something we know we shouldn't, it's wrong. Even if the sin has become habitual or addictive, it is still wrong. Just because you need money doesn't give you permission to steal it. If someone says something mean about you, you don't have the right to say something mean about them. Even if you feel you're in love, it isn't okay for you to have sex until after you are married.

So how can you stop? First and foremost, you are going to have to want to stop. If there is nothing about the sin that bothers you, then you will feel no need to stop doing it. You might try looking into why it is wrong.

Next, get something that reminds you to stop. A bracelet, a ring, a piece of special colored tape put in a strategic location; all these can help remind you to think before you act.

Finally, take one day at a time. Deep-rooted sin is usually not conquered in one day, it takes time. If you can conquer one day at a time, you are on the right road. If you blow it, don't get caught back in the pattern of the sin; start the process again of overcoming the issue.

**Look, men are waiting to ambush me. Cruel men attack me, but I have not sinned or done wrong, LORD.** > > > > > > > > > > > > > > > > > > > > > > > >

**>> Psalm 59:3**

Maybe, just maybe you like working there. It has a bad reputation, but the pay is good, the people you work with are nice, and the work goes by fast. Working in a fast-food restaurant is not for everyone, but you like it.

It is hard to understand why you take so much ridicule for your job, but it happens. At school you are known as "fry-girl" or "greasy cheeks." It isn't very flattering and you put up with it for the most part, but you have to admit that it does hurt to hear those kinds of comments. What really chaps your butt is that a lot of the comments are coming from people you don't even know. They are people who heard someone else put you down, so they join in. They have no idea where you work or who you are! It gets to the point where you don't just feel like the class idiot, you feel like the school idiot. You question why God hasn't helped you.

Have you asked Him to? Write down the names of the people who get to you, irritate you and hurt you. Pray for them by name every day for a week and see what happens with them and your attitude.

Children, come and listen to me. I will teach you to worship the LORD. >>>>>>>>>>>>>>>>

## >> Psalm 34:11

I admit it. I love going to theme parks. I love the roller coasters and all the other rides that you find there. I have been to some in California (like thirty times) and I have never lived in the state! Kinda weird, isn't it? The thing is, I just love to go.

There is something about having a great day doing something that you love. It might not be theme parks for you; it might be camping, skateboarding, concerts—whatever gives you complete joy. If only every day could be as awesome.

If every day isn't that kind of day in your life, try looking at your worship. Worship can be—should be—unbelievably fun and totally captivating. When you get done with worship, you should feel completely full and satisfied.

If you are feeling like your life bites, take a look at how you are worshiping God. It may be the cause of those feelings.

## >> John 11:35

It is probably the most memorized verse in the Bible. No surprise, since it's so short. If you're in some Bible memory contest, this verse always comes in handy. Just two words. And yet, it is also one of the most interesting verses in the Bible. Why? Because it really shows the human side of Jesus. Although He is God, Jesus was also a man, a man filled with emotions. You might think that it's not cool to cry, or that crying is for weak people, but Jesus is one of the strongest men to have lived and He cried. He was so moved with compassion that He shed tears, tears for a friend who had died.

All this to say that it is okay to express sadness in our lives. Maybe it is a movie, the death of a pet, or even something as severe as losing a close family member. It's alright to cry. In fact, it is healthy to cry. It shows the people around you how deeply moved you are by an event. Sometimes words just can't express how you feel, but almost always, tears will. It literally helps you "clean out" your system. If you need to, go ahead and cry. Jesus did and it helped him. This verse may be small, but it is significant.

## John 13:5, 11

Then he poured water into a bowl and began to wash the followers' feet, drying them with the towel that was wrapped around him. Jesus knew who would turn against him, and that is why he said, "Not all of you are clean." >>>>>>>>>

Can you imagine this scenario? Jesus is around the table with His disciples. He pulls out a bowl, water, and a towel, and begins to wash their dirty feet. Here is the Savior of the world washing nasty feet. And I mean nasty. Then you add this: He washed Judas' feet too. And He knew that Judas was about to betray Him. He didn't just suspect that He would be betrayed by Judas, He knew it.

If you had been Jesus, what would you have done? Spit in the water? Skip Judas altogether? Jesus did nothing out of the ordinary for the situation. He washed the feet of Judas just like everyone else. If that isn't unconditional love, what is?

If you were Jesus how would you handle the situation? Think about it. What are your guidelines for love? Write them down on a piece of paper and look them over. Now go to your Bible and look at what the Bible says our guidelines for love should be. Check out Romans 12 and 1 Corinthians 13. Are the lists different or the same?

## >> Ephesians 2:8-9

You hurt as much as anyone does. You have been watching your little sister all year as she played softball. Her team has won the championship and you are so proud. She has had a good year on a good team. After the season, the team votes her the most valuable player. Now your family is really excited. This means that she will be named to the all-star team. You are all going to have a big party to celebrate.

The all-stars are announced at the league picnic. Five members of your sister's team make it, but not your sister. You are mad. As you look at the girls who did make it, they are all girls whose dads coach or umpire the games. Your dad had too many projects at work to be involved this year. Now you realize it isn't what you do, it is who you know.

The same is true of the kingdom of God. It is not how much you do to try and get into the kingdom, it is who you know. Maybe you think that wearing bracelets or having fish stickers on your car gets you to God. Sorry, that has nothing to do with it. What are you doing to try and get closer to God? You gotta know Him.

Then he lay down under the tree and slept. Suddenly an angel came to him and touched him. "Get up and eat," the angel said. Elijah saw near his head a loaf baked over coals and a jar of water, so he ate and drank. Then he went back to sleep. >>>>>>>

This is huge. Your mom is going to pick you up at your best friend's house at midnight, and you'd better be there. After screwing around all night, you run into some unexpected trouble on the way back to her house. Some other friends are stranded on the side of the road with car trouble. Do you stop or do you get home? If your mom gets to your friend's house and you're not there, you are in huge trouble. You are already on thin ice for breaking curfew last weekend, and this could be pushing your luck.

You decide to stop and help. "C'mon, God, if there was ever a time I need You, it is now" is the short, silent prayer you offer up and then just let it go. At about 2:00 A.M. you get home, and your mom is ticked to put it mildly. What could you have done? They were your friends and you couldn't just leave them stranded!

In moments of despair, God does provide, but we also have to take action. Elijah had to wake up to eat, according to the verse. What could you have done to make it to your mom on time or at least have gotten her a message? Good solutions require action.

My dear brothers and sisters, always be willing to listen and slow to speak. Do not become angry easily. > > > > > > > > > > > > > > > > > > > > > > > >

There you are, driving down the road minding your own business when you spot a car in your rearview mirror. It isn't just any car, it is going extremely fast and weaving in and out of traffic like a madman. You stay focused on the road, but you are still watching this maniac out of the corner of your eye. Suddenly they are right beside you with plenty of freeway in front of them. Instead of using the lane they are in, they cut you off. You can't believe it. All you were doing was driving like normal, and they cut you off. Without even thinking, it happens. Your middle finger goes up. You tell yourself they deserved it. Suddenly the car slows down in front of you. Uh oh, now what.

See, sometimes we get mad and do really dumb things, things that can get us into trouble. James made it clear that if you're going to get mad, do it slowly. That is why the whole "counting to ten" works, because it forces you to slow down. When you slow down, you think about why you're mad. Then you respond instead of react. Try counting to ten the next time you find yourself getting angry.

KODAK 5046   8   KODAK 5046 LPP   7   KODAK 5046 LPP

## >> Psalm 46:1-2

God is our protection and our strength. He always helps in times of trouble. So we will not be afraid even if the earth shakes, or the mountains fall into the sea. >>>>>>>>>>>>>>>>>>>>>>>>>

No way around it, just one of those bad days. It was bad from the beginning. First, you slept right through your alarm, waking up 5 minutes before school started. When you hopped into the shower, you discovered that your sister used up all the hot water, so now you're late and cold. You hurry into school and run down the hall, for which the snobbiest teacher in the school gives you detention.

During your first class you get the test back from the week before and find out you failed it. You have no money for lunch, so you are hungry for the rest of the day. As you start to drive home from school, you look at your gas gauge and discover you are out of gas. Only ten seconds later your car comes to a stop and you are dry. With no one to help you, you push the car for three blocks to the gas station and then remember. No money. You scrounge fifty cents out of your seat and get enough gas to get home. You head to the computer to go online and talk with your friends, but your mom has put a lock on the computer. You give up. Does anyone really care about your bad day? It doesn't feel like anyone does. It sounds cheesy, but God does care. Why don't you tell Him about it? He'd love to hear from you.

So you must stop telling lies. Tell each other the truth, because we all belong to each other in the same body. >>>>>>>>>>>>>>>>>>>>>>>

Have you ever had to be completely, maybe even brutally honest with someone? They might have hurt you with something they said, and you need to let them know it. You know that bringing it up will hurt, but if you don't, they'll continue with the same patterns in their life.

Do you just let it go? Do you confront 'em? How? Here is a way to confront in love:

Do it honestly. Plan to say exactly what you mean. Don't try and sugar coat what you are feeling.

When bringing up the issue, keep the focus on you, not them. You don't want to blame them, you just want them to know how you feel about what has happened. Try to not say "you."

Remember that you are not looking for them to apologize to you; you are just trying to tell them how their actions made you feel. It is the work of the Holy Spirit to convict them.

If you expect an apology, you'll probably be disappointed, so keep the focus on you, not them.

## >> Matthew 9:10-12

As Jesus was having dinner at Matthew's house, many tax collectors and "sinners" came and ate with Jesus and his followers. When the Pharisees saw this, they asked Jesus' followers, "Why does your teacher eat with tax collectors and sinners?" When Jesus heard them, he said, "It is not the healthy people who need a doctor, but the sick."

>>>>>>>>>>>>>>>>>>>>>>>>>>>>>>>

You really need a little sin by your life. Notice I didn't say that you need a little sin *in* your life, just *by* it. It's good for you to be around people that are ungodly.

You might go to a Christian school, have all Christian friends, go to church five nights a week, and play in a Christian band. Those are all great things, but they are not effective in building God's kingdom. We can't expect people who have no relationship with God, or people who think of God as irrelevant, to come to us. We need to go to them. We need to be around these people and not overreact to their world.

If you look at the life of Jesus, He was always around those people who really needed Him. He was the model for us to follow.

If you don't have any friends who don't believe in God, or who don't value a relationship with God, then go get some. You need to have these people around you so you can understand how to share the story of God with them.

> In the same way, the Son of Man did not come to be served. He came to serve others and to give his life as a ransom for many people. > > > > > > > > > > > >

## >> Matthew 20:28

Call the Salvation Army and find out when their next food drive or other event is happening. Volunteer to help them out for the entire day. Then try something bold: Get as many friends to go with you as you can.

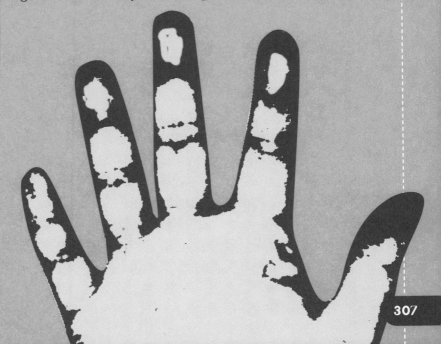

Teach us how short our lives really are so that we may be wise. >>>>>>>>>>>>>>>>>>>>>>>

## >> Psalm 90:12

Do you realize how short our lives really are? In light of human history, we are barely a little blip on the screen. But it doesn't matter how little time we have as long as we take advantage of that time. Look at a small list of people who were here for a short time but still made a huge impact: Martin Luther King Jr., Abraham Lincoln, Jesus, William Shakespeare, the list goes on.

Understand this: We don't have as much time as we might think! We must take full advantage of the time that we are given. You can make a huge impact with a little effort.

First, be wise in the way that you spend your time. It is okay to be a couch or computer potato sometimes, but is that how you really want to spend your life? Second, make it a practice to share Jesus with one person each day. You could tell the salesperson at the convenience store that you are on your way to a church function as a way to bring up God. Talk at lunch about how you see God working in your life. Do anything that gets God noticed in a positive way, that helps people respond to Him.

It is easy if you apply yourself. You can make a difference for God every day, starting now.

"So when you pray, you should pray like this: 'Our Father in heaven, may your name always be kept holy." >>>>>>>>>>>>>>>>>>>>>>>>>>

## >> Matthew 6:9

Here is a simple little prayer taken from what we traditionally call the "Lord's Prayer." Pray this when you can't think of anything else to pray for.

*Heavenly Father, may your name always be set apart. As my life in You unfolds, please show me the way that You want me to go while I am here on earth, until the day I stand before You. Please provide for all of my needs so that I rely on no one but You. Forgive me for the times that I feel I don't need You, and help me to forgive those I need to forgive. As I get tempted in life, help me to find the way out that only You can provide so that Satan doesn't catch me in one of his traps.*

Like any prayer, make it from your heart, that's what God wants to hear about. Jesus gave us a model to help us convey what our hearts feel and need to tell God. Take some time right now to think through the prayers of your heart.

309

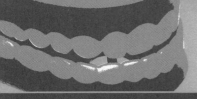

> Brothers and sisters, we want you to know about those Christians who have died so you will not be sad, as others who have no hope. ⟩⟩⟩⟩⟩⟩⟩

## ⟩⟩ 1 Thessalonians 4:13

It's something that no one likes to talk about, not in a real sense. We like to think of it as something that is far off—something we don't have to think about until we are really old. DEATH.

There are people who say they can't wait to die, because then they will be in the presence of God. Sounds nice, right? But to most people, even Christians, the thought of death is a little scary. The fear might come from thinking about life in this world going on without you. Maybe you won't get married, or have kids, or even grandkids before you die. We think about all that we stand to lose. And that focus just might be the problem.

Instead of thinking about what you will be missing out on, think about the benefits of death as a Christian. Yes, we may miss out on some experiences in this world, but what we will get in return will far outweigh those things we leave behind. Think about it, in the presence of God! The God who cares for us on this earth, constantly with us. It won't be a freaky thing; it will be fun. Thinking about how it will be for us as Christians when we die, as opposed to the alternative, should give us a lot of hope and curb our fear.

## >> Romans 12:3

Because God has given me a special gift, I have something to say to everyone among you. Do not think you are better than you are. You must decide what you really are by the amount of faith God has given you. > > > > > > > > > > > > > > > > > > > >

How should Christians act? Should you be able to pick them out of a crowd? Should a Christian blend into his or her environment? When someone comes to faith in Jesus, should they automatically put a WWJD bracelet on? Should a person change their life *then* come to faith in Jesus or does it work the other way around? If we are all saved by grace, should we change anything in our life at all?

All of these are good questions, and you might have thought about them many times. But maybe you've been too scared to ask them—for fear of looking stupid to those who believe they have all the answers.

The Bible does tell us to be set apart as Christians, but in a way that draws people into the kingdom of God, not in ways that make people want to stay away from Him.

Think about how you treat people who are not Christians. How about those who are "baby" Christians. Evaluate your motives. Are you trying to make them like *you* or helping them discover who *they* are in Christ? As Christians, we give direction. We are not called to make clones of ourselves.

Help the people in your life discover who they are in Christ. Who knows, you might learn something about yourself as well!

311

Give me back the joy of your salvation. Keep me strong by giving me a willing spirit. >>>>>>>

>> Psalm 51:12

You didn't mean for it to happen, but it did. You tried your hardest to protect yourself from it. But it still happened. Friends warned you that it might happen and you just blew them off. "That won't happen to me," you said. But it did. You get frustrated when you see others with it and you start realizing that you had it once, but now it is gone. And now you are skeptical when you see someone else find theirs after losing it for a while. It's making you crazy! You're not supposed to lose something this valuable! Then you read in your Bible that it happens to the best of us. David wrote that he lost it and needed it restored.

I'm talking about "the joy of God's salvation." That overwhelming sense of pure delight that you experienced when you first had faith in God, or when you were walking with Him very closely. What happened? How could you lose that kind of joy? There could be a thousand reasons why you lost it. The better question is "How do I get it back?" No easy answer. Start by asking God to help you, like David did.

Next, look for that joy in the ordinary things of life. Find ways to make your faith fun. A sure way to experience it: Watch someone come to the realization that they need God. Watch their joy—hopefully it will rub off.

As you received Christ Jesus the Lord, so continue to live in him. Keep your roots deep in him and have your lives built on him. >>>>>>>>>>>>>>

Sometimes it can be very discouraging to be a Christian. Rob found that out as his life in Christ developed. He loves his relationship with God because it gives him fulfillment in life—he feels like his life matters. But Rob gets discouraged thinking that he doesn't know very much. He sits in Bible study, and when the group gets asked to look up a verse in the Bible, everyone turns to the right place. Rob still has to use the table of contents. Rob can't spout off John 3:16 from memory, and he has trouble understanding the difference between the Old Testament and the New Testament.

The thing Rob needs to realize is that it doesn't matter how much he knows. What matters is Who he knows. He knows and loves God. The knowledge will come with time. Comparing what we know with what others know is a waste of time. We will always run into someone who knows more, but that shouldn't keep us from learning.

Rob made a pact with himself. He would keep asking questions and seeking answers regardless of how others made him feel. He knew that would be the only way to learn the right direction.

## >> Exodus 20:15

It is an awful dilemma to be in, but what do you do? You walk out of Abercrombie with your friend, and about 15 minutes later she shows you the T-shirt she ripped off from the store. You know what she did was wrong, but how do you bring it up? She is a close friend and you don't want to jeopardize the friendship, so you just let it go.

The next time you go to the mall with her, you actually watch her steal a pair of gloves. Now there is a real feeling in your heart that you need to do something, but it's so hard. If you let it go and she gets caught, you will be guilty by association. If you confront her, you might lose her friendship.

You finally get your nerves about you and call her on it. You have thought through exactly what you want to say. You commit yourself to talking to her the way you would want to be talked to if you were the one being confronted. You tell her that she needs to stop or she could end up getting into big trouble—a fine, a record, even jail-type of trouble. You also tell her that if she chooses to continue stealing, you will have to make the choice of not hanging out with her anymore, especially not going to the mall.

Don't let that kind of stuff go by unchallenged! The sinner is not only victimizing himself—he is hurting others with his actions. It may not be popular, but it is the right thing to do. Doing what is right isn't always popular, just ask Jesus.

Jesus answered, "If people love me, they will obey my teaching. My Father will love them, and we will come to them and make our home with them."

> > > > > > > > > > > > > > > > > > > > > > > > > > > > > >

You actually got to meet *NSYNC. You still can't believe it! They actually took time out of their day to talk with you. You work at the local arena and knew you had a decent chance of running into them. This is the band you have always wanted to meet. They said hi to you, and you were even fortunate enough to have your picture taken with them.

The next day at school you told everyone you came into contact with. Some were extremely impressed, while others were embarrassed for you. The picture was proof, and for the next two weeks you were talking about *NSYNC with anyone who would listen.

About a month later the band isn't as hot as they once were, and the magic of getting to meet them has rubbed off. Besides, since meeting them, you have had no contact with them at all. In reality, they probably don't even remember you exist.

This same experience sometimes happens with God. We go to a camp, retreat, or conference and get all fired up about our relationship with Him, only to have that fire fade once we get home. The difference is this: God still knows you exist and loves you just as much. You can be assured of that because of what His word says. Develop your relationship by continuing to spend time with Him daily, not just at retreats and camps. We might move, but God won't.

> I gave them food, and they became full and satisfied. But then they became too proud and forgot me. >>

## >> Hosea 13:6

Pride is an awful thing. This is what pride can do if left alone: Sever relationships because someone refuses to apologize. Keep missionaries from going because they don't want to ask for money. Stop friendships because we can't see beyond the mirror. Break up families because siblings are unwilling to look at themselves realistically. Create school violence because someone feels disrespected. End a life because someone got passed on the freeway and they had to prove themselves. Flunk a test out of fear of asking a stupid question in front of the class. Destroy a life because someone craved a high. Kill brain cells in the name of finding a new reality. Split churches and ministries because God's people refuse to seek solutions. Cause us to walk in spiritual darkness because we fail to acknowledge our need for God.

What issues of pride do you need to give up now? Write out what your issues are and ask God to deal with each of the areas, one at a time. Don't let pride destroy your life.

> **But these are written so that you may believe that Jesus is the Christ, the Son of God. Then, by believing, you may have life through his name.** >>

## >> John 20:31

You have been reading devotional books, like this one, for quite a while now. You enjoy reading these because they are quick, easy, and to the point. Now you would like just a little bit more, but where do you start? I think the easiest way to start is to simply dive more into your Bible. Start by reading the Gospels because they will give you a clear picture of the words Jesus said. You might go to your local Christian bookstore and find a Bible study that will guide you with some simple questions. This might help you think in different ways about what you are reading. Maybe even get a simple Bible commentary to help explain some of the passages that are difficult to understand. Use any tool available to help you get to know God better through the words that He wrote.

Be consistent, reading through Matthew, Mark, Luke, and John. After that, ask your pastor what he might recommend you read. God loves that you are interested about what He has to say. As you read, you'll develop an interest in who He is.

All the people who heard him were amazed. They said, "This is the man who was in Jerusalem trying to destroy those who trust in this name! He came here to arrest the followers of Jesus and take them back to the leading priests." > > > > > > > > > >

Want to watch how much you change over the years? Do this. Write yourself a letter. Write it as if you were writing it to another person, but knowing that one day you will read it. When you're done, seal it in an envelope and give it to your parents. Ask them to return the letter to you in five to ten years. Then, when you look back after reading the letter, you will see how much you have changed. Will those changes be positive or negative?